Video Journalism for the Web

As newspapers and broadcast news outlets direct more resources toward online content, print reporters and photojournalists are picking up video cameras and crafting new kinds of stories with their lenses. Creating multimedia video journalism requires more than simply adapting traditional broadcast techniques: it calls for a new way of thinking about how people engage with the news and with emerging media technologies. In this guide, Kurt Lancaster teaches students and professional journalists how to shoot better video and tell better stories on the web, providing a strong understanding of cinematic storytelling and documentary production so their videos will stand out from the crowd.

Video Journalism for the Web introduces students to all the basic skills and techniques of good video journalism and documentary storytelling, from shots and camera movements to sound and editing—as well as offering tips for developing compelling, character-driven narratives and using social media to launch a successful career as a "backpack journalist." Shooting, editing, and writing exercises throughout the book allow students to put these techniques into practice, and case studies and interviews with top documentary journalists provide real-world perspectives on a career in video journalism. This book gives aspiring documentary journalists the tools they need to get out in the field and start shooting unforgettable multimedia stories.

Kurt Lancaster is the author of *DSLR Cinema: Crafting the Film Look with Video*. He is an associate professor at Northern Arizona University where he teaches digital filmmaking and multimedia journalism in the School of Communication.

Video Journalism for the Web

A Practical Introduction to Documentary Storytelling

Kurt Lancaster
Northern Arizona University

 Routledge
Taylor & Francis Group

NEW YORK AND LONDON

First published 2013
by Routledge
711 Third Avenue, New York, NY 10017

Simultaneously published in the UK
by Routledge
2 Park Square, Milton Park, Abingdon, Oxon OX14 4RN

Routledge is an imprint of the Taylor & Francis Group, an informa business

Library of Congress Cataloging in Publication Data
Lancaster, Kurt, 1967–.
 Video journalism for the web: a practical introduction to documentary
 storytelling/by Kurt Lancaster.
 p. cm.
 "Simultaneously published in the UK."
 Includes index.
 1. Documentary films—Production and direction. 2. Video journalism.
 3. Online journalism. 4. Digital video. 5. Journalism—Authorship.
 6. Reporters and reporting. 7. Journalism—Technological innovations.
 8. Journalists—Interviews. I. Title. II. Title: Documentary storytelling.
 PN1995.9.D6L365 2012
 070.1—dc23
 2011051860

ISBN: 978-0-415-89266-7 (hbk)
ISBN: 978-0-415-89267-4 (pbk)
ISBN: 978-0-203-14575-3 (ebk)

Typeset in Aldine401 BT and Helvetica Neue by
Florence Production Ltd, Stoodleigh, Devon

Printed and bound in the United States of America
by Edwards Brothers, Inc.

For Stephanie Petrie, my guiding star

Contents

Figures

Foreword

This is the most exciting moment there has ever been for a storyteller. Both the production of and appetite for good stories is exploding.

Fueled by cheaper and more powerful tools, everyone has the ability to gather and distribute their stories now. Because of these changes, documentary journalists can have authorship and reach.

How stories are delivered is not as relevant as it was in the past. People will still watch TV, they will still read, but they will also consume stories on tablets, on their mobile phones, and on platforms that are only now emerging.

Even with all the change, the fundamentals of a great story remain and that's why this book is so useful.

Lancaster's writing, interviews, and real-world examples will give you a great launch pad for advancing your work as a documentary journalist.

Storytelling skills have been honed and refined for years in traditional media. We need to bring forward and integrate the best of each discipline—the ambient style of great radio together with the sophisticated compositions of still photography and the lyrical motion of documentary video.

Enjoy this book and your journey as a storyteller.

Brian Storm
Founder and Executive Producer, MediaStorm
http://mediastorm.com

Acknowledgments

I am grateful for the assistance of Northern Arizona University's Faculty Development grant that allowed me to research this project in the summer of 2009, covering my trips to Mexicali, Mexico, and New York City.

The following people opened up and shared their lives and experiences with me through interviews: Ann Derry of the *New York Times*, Jigar Mehta, formerly of the *New York Times*, Bill Gentile of American University, the Renaud Brothers, Jimmy Orr of the *Los Angeles Times*, Angela Morris, a freelance video journalist, Wes Pope, a veteran of photo- and multimedia journalism, John Yemma, the editor of the *Christian Science Monitor*, Ellen Spiro from the University of Texas, Austin, Brian Storm of mediastorm.com, multimedia storyteller Bob Sacha, and especially Travis Fox, formerly of the *Washington Post*, who allowed me to travel in the field and observe him working. Many of the examples from this book are drawn from his work.

My special thanks to Stephanie Petrie for traveling with me to Mexicali—her assistance was invaluable.

I wish to also thank my editor, Erica Wetter and her assistant Margo Irvin, who helped me shepherd this book along. Erica was instrumental in pushing me into restructuring the book into its current form, and I thank her for it.

My colleagues at Northern Arizona University's School of Communication, where I teach multimedia journalism and digital filmmaking, have all been supportive: Mark Neumann, Laura Camden, Peter Friederici, Mary Tolan, Marty Sommerness, Annette McGivney, Wes Pope, Kate Szrom, Rory Faust, Paul Helford, Norm Medoff, Charlie Hicks, Brandon Neuman, Dale Hoskins, Jon Torn, and Janna Jones.

COPYRIGHT

Images from "Mexico at War: Journey along the Border with Travis Fox and William Booth" produced by Travis Fox with William Booth reproduced by permission of the *Washington Post*. Copyright © 2009.

Image from "Salton Sea Beach" produced by Philip Bloom reproduced by permission of the producer. Copyright © 2010. philipbloom.co.uk.

Images from "Bill Cagle is a 24-Year AIDS Survivor" produced by Wes Pope courtesy the *San Francisco Chronicle*. Copyright © 2011.

Introduction

What is Documentary Journalism?

WHY MORE VIDEO?

This book teaches the reader how to shoot better video and tell better stories by learning from those who practice some of the best techniques in the field—whether you are a reporter trained in a conventional broadcast news style, a photographer who has been asked by an editor if she can shoot some video for the newspaper's website, a print journalist who never imagined that they would be "writing" stories with a video camera rather than their word processor, or perhaps your paper no longer exists in print—but it's now online and you need video to engage an audience wanting more multimedia. Or you may even be a top journalist that saw her paper fold and you went freelance—you're a strong writer, but you have a feeling you could become entrepreneurial and set up a blog where you can write and put up video to help attract an audience. Perhaps you're a student thinking about going into journalism or you're already enrolled in J-school and you're being told that you need to do multimedia if you ever hope to enter the profession.

By showing practicing journalists and journalism students how to create short, but strong, nonfiction video for the web, this book hopes to become the teacher in guiding you to craft stronger video stories. I show in Chapter 1 how a documentary style engages cinematic conventions in structuring a story and how it differs greatly from the style engaged by video journalists working for conventional broadcast news.[1] I call video journalists shooting in a cinematic style "documentary journalists."

This doesn't mean it's the end of broadcast news. It will keep its form for television, because it works within the given structured format, and many television news websites upload their broadcasts online. But it's healthy in a democracy to express video news in different forms. Photojournalists and print journalists are picking up video cameras and crafting new kinds of stories with their lenses, stories more closely attuned to their documentary film cousins than to their broadcast news siblings.

This book celebrates and closely analyzes some of the examples found at newspaper websites, revealing the differences in style between broadcast news and documentary journalism. Brian Storm, the founder and president of mediastorm.com—one of the primary leaders in online visual journalism today—notes how this documentary style includes the primary use of the subject's voice, instead of the reporter's voice we see so often in the conventional broadcast news style:

> it's just refreshing to hear the subject of a story tell you their story as opposed to some beautiful television person telling you . . . standing in front of the situation saying this is what you should be seeing and what you should be thinking. I don't feel we need that (Junnarkar 2007).

Although the conventional broadcast style is important, it is not the only style—so I tend to agree with Storm that it is refreshing to discover other forms of video journalism, and this book was written in order to closely examine some of the best works of video journalism engaging in the documentary style.

Video Journalism for the Web includes analysis of videos by the Emmy Award-winning Travis Fox, formerly of the *Washington Post*, one of the top video journalists working today. It also includes work by such dynamic video journalists as Jigar Mehta, formerly of the *New York Times*, and Adam Ellick, a print reporter from the *New York Times*, who is now one of their best video journalists. In no way are my examples exhaustive. You can go to nearly any documentary story on mediastorm.com and learn from some of the masters (take a look at Danny Wilcox Frazier's "Driftless: Stories from Iowa" for a great example of documentary journalism). It's impossible for this book to survey or analyze everyone's work. I'm looking at a few examples that, to me, represent some of the best in the field, and I use them as case studies so that others can learn from master documentary journalists.

This is the kind of book I was looking for when asked to train print reporters for the Pulitzer Prize-winning international paper, the *Christian Science Monitor*—one of the first to drop their print daily and go online. It is really for those who have never picked up a video camera, but are being asked to do two jobs—write a text story and produce video—as well as for those who are shooting video but are not quite sure how to make their work better.

Whatever the shooting style, the documentary form of journalism is not one necessarily designed to garner high ratings—which usually typify sensationally crafted disaster reports, political fights with little to no analysis, celebrity news, and talk-show hosts masquerading as journalists as they are more concerned about manipulating an audience's emotions rather than engaging in critical thinking. A "call to arms" against such "journalism," this book is designed for video journalists who want to craft thoughtful, character-driven pieces—the documentary journalists who are given the time and give the time to let their characters speak, who step back from personality and instead send back images of integrity and honesty about everyday citizens struggling and finding hope in a transnational, postmodern world.

MORE THAN TWO SIDES TO A STORY

Documentary filmmaker Ellen Spiro (*Body of War*, 2007; *Troop 1500*, 2005; *Atomic Ed & the Black Hole*, 2003) challenges the notion of there being only two sides to a story, a construction of point and counterpoint designed to artificially build a sense of conflict to a story: "I believe there's a kaleidoscope of perspectives on any given issue," Spiro contends (interview with author, 2009). I feel that many video journalists are beginning to find and present these "kaleidoscopes of perspectives," providing audiences with a wider perspective to stories.

Furthermore, Spiro argues that the quickly produced news story—with reporters dropping in for such little time due to tight deadlines—often results in a side-effect of "not having empathy." Persons shown in tragic situations, she explains, shot by someone not having empathy, "desensitizes us to real human problems and tragedies and it makes people less likely to intervene to solve the problems that we face as a society." So the larger question this book explores includes the role of the journalist in society. Can we create better, character-centered stories that challenge their audience to be more socially aware, more politically conscious in how the world works, whether we're shooting for online newspapers or for broadcast news?

WHAT'S IN THE BOOK

In *Video Journalism for the Web*, I structure the book around the general principles I teach in my video production classes at Northern Arizona University, while showing examples of some of the best video journalism pieces found on the web—so in many ways it's a classroom in a book. It includes:

- An exploration of the differences—and similarities—of style between documentary journalism and broadcast news. This will set the foundation for the rest of the book, as students can directly see how some video journalists approach a story in different ways.
- Story and character. How do you find a story? How stories should be driven from our passions.
- Crafting images through cinematography techniques. I feel video journalism should look as good as cinema. I also include examples of lighting in natural light situations.
- Interviewing and scriptwriting. I provide an example from one of my pieces of how I approached an interview and then how I created a script from a transcript of interviews. Those with years of experience and a honed sense of storytelling skills may not write a script, but, for the beginner, creating a paper edit from a transcript of interviews provides an easy way to shape the rough cut of your story that you've already shot. It gives your work discipline.
- Editing for rhythm. The edit is not only how the story gets told in video, but it also determines the pacing and rhythm of a story—it could actually determine whether a story lacks energy or expresses verve.
- Sound design. Sound isn't just an add-on. It's not just the dialogue of your characters. It's the underpinning atmosphere of your story, designed to shape the emotional tone.
- The place of blogging in telling several video journalism stories revolving around a single theme.
- As interludes between chapters, I provide interviews with some of the top video and multimedia journalists and editors today.

In Chapter 1, **Differences in Style: Documentary Journalism versus Broadcast News—A Comparative Analysis of a Similar Story at CNN versus the New York Times**, I explore the differences in style between documentary journalism and broadcast news. In CNN's "Girl Poet Takes on the Taliban with Her Pen" and the *New York Times'* "Class Dismissed in Swat Valley," I examine how both stories profile two different eleven-year-old girls in Pakistan—both of whom struggle against the Taliban's desire to force the girls out of schools. The chapter examines the structure of each story, including a summary of each, how the subject is presented, the place of the journalist in the work, how visuals are used to engage the story (including the kinds of shots used), and how narration is used.

With this basic understanding covered, the rest of the book will provide the tools necessary for the video journalist to engage in documentary-style journalism.

In Chapter 2, **Finding a Story and Shaping the Structure: Starting with Character in Jigar Mehta's "The Recession-Proof Artist,"** I examine the classic story structure and how it relates to character by using Mehta's work that he shot and edited for the *New York Times*. It includes a set of basic questions to ask before pursuing a story, and a shot analysis of how he structured his story around character.

Chapter 3, **Shooting the Image: Composition and Lighting in Travis Fox's "Narcocorridos and Nightlife in Mexicali" and "Crisis in Darfur Expands,"** covers the foundation of visual storytelling, providing an examination of the cinematic techniques required to shoot good documentary journalism. In Fox's first example, I'll provide an overview of such cinematic techniques as shot sizes, camera angles, and camera movement. In the Darfur piece, I'll look at how Fox's cinematography, including three-point lighting techniques with natural lighting, is utilized to create a visually compelling work.

In Chapter 4, **Conducting Interviews and Writing a Script: A Workshop with "Icarus Refried: A Pro-Creative Process,"** I include a transcript of one of the interviews I conducted with a performer in a performance art piece I shot in order to show my process in conducting interviews. I then show how I crafted a script from the interviews of the two performers, and how I wove these interviews into the visual material I shot of the performance art piece. This will provide ways to think about how the video journalist can draft a script as a step—a paper edit—before engaging in a rough cut of their material.

Chapter 5, **Editing for Rhythm: Travis Fox's "Redefining China's Family: Women,"** is an exploration of how Fox crafted a dramatic story revolving around a central character through editing. I examine the styles of editing Fox engages when shaping the rhythm and pacing of his work, particularly how he shapes the ebb and flow of changing rhythms in his edit.

In Chapter 6, **Getting Clean Audio and Crafting a Sound Design: An Audio Workshop with Philip Bloom, Travis Fox, and Wes Pope**, I lay out some of the general principles in getting clean audio and the importance of shaping a sound design for your work. Without audio, half the project is missing. The visuals should be strong, but as much attention should be applied to recording clean audio and shaping a compelling sound design. Ultimately, the sound design helps shape the tone of a video journalism piece for an audience. Although I include a couple of brief case studies with Travis Fox and Philip Bloom, the main focus in this chapter comes from video journalist Wes Pope and how he not only gathers audio in the field, but also how he thinks about sound design in the edit.

In Chapter 7, **The Blogging Journalist: Travis Fox and the Mexican Border Stories**, I cover how he and journalist William Booth traveled along the Mexican border in the summer of 2009 to examine the impact of the drug war as told through a series of written work and video blogs for the *Washington Post*.

WHAT ABOUT EQUIPMENT?

As a backpack journalist in the digital age, the options for getting equipment are stupendous—almost too many to even decipher. With the release of DSLRs that shoot high-definition video—such as Canon's Rebel T2i for around $600—you can not only take good photos, but also shoot cinematic quality video. Indeed, the image quality is better than most prosumer-level video cameras costing thousands more. Spend another $500–600, and you can record professional audio with a good microphone and digital audio recorder. Or should you use a consumer video camera or a high-end $6000 camera?

See the following website, located at www.kurtlancaster.com/equipment/, for the author's recommendation of equipment. The equipment listed is certainly not exhaustive, and is chosen based on budget and portability—I will not be recommending any large broadcast journalism cameras that sit on your shoulder, for example, which are designed for a reporter–camera operator team. Documentary journalism is about traveling light and shooting solo.

Go online to package out the best equipment for your needs. However, no matter what equipment you get—whether the least expensive or no-holds-barred—storytelling is the most important tool you'll ever command. As video journalist Travis Fox notes, it's not about equipment, but story. "The film-like DSLR cameras and lenses mixed with new lightweight cinematic tools such as the pocket dolly and mini-jib" may allow for cinematic camera movement—but that doesn't change the fundamentals of journalism, he explains. "For me, it's simple. The journalism part of video journalism or documentary film is about the story. The story is made up of several aspects: the visuals, the writing, the characters, the editing, etc. So if the visuals change—let's say improve—how does that alone change the story, the journalism?" (Fox 2010).

An audience will more likely watch a compelling story shot with mediocre equipment than the best-looking shots failing to deliver a solid story.

PURPOSE OF THE BOOK

By reading this book, I hope you will grasp a stronger sense of storytelling structure as well as learning how to get good-looking shots. Fundamentally, I wrote this book so students and professionals can engage better story techniques by looking at some of the best work produced by video journalists, and, from their work, others can learn how to engage such techniques to improve their stories and shots. The foundational qualities of the journalist do not change by "writing" in different media. As John Yemma, the editor of the *Monitor*, notes: "reporting, curiosity, courage in trying to find something, documenting the evidence, and then telling the story in a compelling way—those are really the fundamentals." This book will focus on these qualities in documentary journalists and how those fundamentals are practiced by them.

CHAPTER 1

Differences in Style

Documentary Journalism versus Broadcast News—A Comparative Analysis of a Similar Story at CNN versus the New York Times

INTRODUCTION TO DOCUMENTARY JOURNALISM

In this chapter, I show the differences between documentary and broadcast news styles by examining two different news stories completed in the broadcast news style and similar stories produced by video journalists working at newspapers. I explore how the style engaged by documentary journalists tends to be character-centered and contain shots that move the story forward visually, while the broadcast style utilizes reporters' narrations instead of the characters' voices as the primary means of crafting their stories, with shots tending to be more utilitarian rather than cinematic.

If documentary journalism is more cinematic, engages deeper character studies, and supports strong visual journalism, then why isn't it utilized more often in the broadcast style? The advantages of the broadcast news style—it's fast and simple:

- It can be produced quickly (and, when on a deadline, that's imperative); while, in documentary journalism, more time is needed to produce a piece.
- A wide-range of audience types can quickly grasp the story and get it in a short attention span, and if they're cooking dinner, they can still hear the story, since it relies primarily on narration; in documentary journalism the audience is required to watch the story, often needing to pay close attention to capture its nuances.

Ultimately, viewers may end up determining which style becomes more prevalent. Right now, newspapers are in a position to experiment with a variety of news styles online. Broadcast news stations are fixed in their style by tradition and decades of making it work. They could express different styles online, but it requires additional resources. Regardless, I offer this analysis as a way for students and practitioners of visual journalism to think about how they approach their stories, and to help those shooting and producing broadcast news to think about how they might approach their work more cinematically, with more attention to visual storytelling and character presentation.

HOW TO TELL THE DIFFERENCE BETWEEN TV NEWS AND DOCUMENTARY JOURNALISM STYLES

The case studies below will clearly show the differences in style, but this list summarizes some of the primary elements of the two. It's not a cut-and-dried formulaic list, but, in general, it is what distinguishes the two styles:

TV News Style

- TV reporter often in front of the camera.
- Character secondary to the reporter's presence.
- Reporter's narration the primary means in telling the story.
- Character's voice used to augment the reporter's narration.
- Images used to illustrate the story.
- Audio captured in the field as the only audio used.
- Camera operated by a crew member, guided by the reporter and/or producer.

Documentary Journalism Style

- Journalist behind the camera.
- Character primary.
- Reporter's narration, if used, provides context.
- Character's voice utilized to tell the story.
- Images show the story cinematically.
- Audio consciously designed to help set the tone.
- Video journalist usually works alone and uses the camera to write the story, visually.

CASE STUDY 1—"GIRL POET TAKES ON THE TALIBAN WITH HER PEN" (2:37) BY STANLEY GRANT, CNN (FEB. 18, 2009)

www.cnnstudentnews.cnn.com/2009/WORLD/asiapcf/02/17/pakistan.girl.poet/index.html

The stories were selected randomly. Ellick's and Sharaf's documentary was on the main video page of the *New York Times*, and I was compelled to watch it all the way through. This is my way of saying that I'm not purposely looking for broadcast news work that stands in contrast to the documentaries I found at online newspaper sites. But it was a serendipitous search, allowing me to explore how the two different styles work.

First, let's look at CNN's "Girl Poet Takes on the Taliban with Her Pen" and compare it with Case Study 2, the *New York Times*'s "Class Dismissed in Swat Valley." In each story, there is a profile of an eleven-year-old girl living in Pakistan: one in Islamabad, the other in the Swat valley region. Both struggle against the Taliban's desire to force girls out of schools. Over two hundred schools for girls have been destroyed in Pakistan by the Taliban.

In Grant's "Girl Poet Takes on the Taliban with Her Pen," we see the story of Tuba Sahaab, a girl fighting for the right to an education as the Taliban try to prevent her and other girls from attending school.

The story is inspiring and it captures the heart of the audience in just over two and half minutes. We feel for Tuba and her plight. The cinematography is strong, especially shots 8–14, where visual elements capture Tuba's desire and personality. The zoom-in with Grant sitting next to her, as we go to the final shot of her face, touches the heart. Yet, with all due respect to Grant's hard work on this inspiring piece, by placing the reporter at the center of the story, his personality dominates, and not that of Tuba Sahaab—he's the figure that draws the United States audience in, he's the character we can relate to, as he talks about Tuba and her accomplishments, his narration providing the story, the story needing few, if any, visuals to inform the audience of its content. If we read the transcript, we can see that the visual shots only supplement the story and offer little in helping to reveal deeper story elements.

Grant frames the story around Tuba's hopes for President Barack Obama to help set her country right. From the opening narration—"President Obama, you have won a young heart in Pakistan," Grant laughs with personality. Shot 3, with a series of questions and answers revolving around Tuba's excitement about Obama becoming president, sets up her desire and hope—but it is a bit disingenuous, since Grant and his audience know it's highly unlikely that Obama will be able to do anything about her plight. Even if unintentional, she is framed as being naïve, and his lines at the end—"I think you'll get a chance . . . there's no doubt what you can do"—encapsulate the American ideal—the American Dream—voiced paternally to a "daughter" who may, in fact, be overreaching the bounds of her own safety. Grant becomes the figure by which she, perhaps, sets up her hopes. What happens if there is no response?

The story focuses on a central character with a story, and it is shot well—meeting the standards of good documentary filmmaking. Ultimately, however, this style lacks Tuba's voice. Rather, Grant's personality takes over the piece and he becomes the central character by which we vicariously experience Tuba's emotions, struggles, dreams, and hopes. We don't feel invited into her world and it becomes filtered through Grant as our host to Tuba's world. For a package created for CNN, the television news style works for what it needs to do—convey a story quickly and in an entertaining way without going deep into the underlying political issues.

Let's contrast this story to a similar one done for the *New York Times*, this one produced in a documentary style.

CASE STUDY 2—"CLASS DISMISSED IN SWAT VALLEY" (14:24) BY ADAM B. ELLICK AND IRFAN ASHRAF, THE *NEW YORK TIMES* (FEB. 21, 2009)

http://video.nytimes.com/video/2009/02/22/world/1194838044017/class-dismissed-in-swat-valley.html

Ellick and Ashraf tell the story of an eleven-year-old girl and her father living in Swat valley, a hundred miles from Islamabad. It is 5.4 times longer than the CNN piece, so there's time for the journalists to explore their subject in depth, so perhaps it's an unfair comparison. Yet, in order to create strong visual journalism, it's important to look at the differences in style, which can be utilized for nearly any length.

Despite the length of the piece, Ellick engages a documentary style, a style far different than the one produced by Stanley Grant for CNN. The main difference involves the amount of time Ellick and Ashraf spent with this family—forty-eight hours documenting them right before the Taliban ordered the closure of the schools for girls in the Swat valley region. The narration provides historical and political context, and includes file footage of battles, Taliban whipping people into submission, and beheaded bodies. The images visually drive home the point that the fear the family experiences is real. Their story may not be exhaustive, but it expresses political context and contains the information needed to understand the family's predicament. In the CNN piece, I feel pushed into it through a rapid narrated style that tells me what to think, taking the story at face value, while the *New York Times* piece—although guiding us with narration—feels more like an invitation into the story, taking us deeper into the emotions that circulate among the characters.

In sequence one, comprising just under the first minute (0:00–0:57), we see eight shots: images of Swat valley, an Islamic flag, followed by the sounds of gunfire and the images of burning and shooting. We hear the father, Sahudeem, talk about how "there are some people who want to stop educating girls through guns," followed by his daughter talking about wanting to become a doctor. The shot stays on the two for a few moments (shot 7), then cuts to a close-up as the daughter, Mulala, covers her face, the emotional truth of the Taliban's will overwhelming her (shot 8).

See Figures 1.1 and 1.2.

In many ways, the CNN and the *New York Times* stories are the same—two eleven-year-old girls struggling with the idea that education could be lost to them if the Taliban get their way. The characters speak in their own voice, but in the first minute of the *Times* piece the only reporter-voiced narration we hear is: "In Swat, Pakistan, schools for girls are under assault by the Taliban." The rest of it involves file footage and a narration provided by the father and a dramatic hook as we hear Mulala speak about her desire to become a doctor. The moment doesn't feel rushed and we don't feel the reporter's voice guiding us along through the story, as seen in the CNN piece—where we get the reporter's voice right away, Grant's onscreen presence becoming the dominant figure in the piece, our guide into Tuba's world. Ellick and Ashraf, on the other hand, let the father and daughter be the central characters, the reporter's presence unfelt, and the narration remains fairly unobtrusive.

Figures 1.1 and 1.2 Shots 7 and 8. Adam Ellick cuts to a close-up of Mulala, as her father, Sahudeem, consoles her in "Class Dismissed in Swat Valley" from *The New York Times* (Courtesy *The New York Times.* ©2009 Used with permission.)

In a later sequence (7:50–9:24, shots 40–54), we can see the main difference between the two styles—which I'll call reporter-personality vs. hybrid cinéma vérité.[2] In Grant's story, the reporter stands as the central character, the guide who takes us by the hand and tells us the story; shots usually move us from one moment to the next in quick succession as determined by the narration, rarely allowing the audience to stay on a particular moment and rarely letting the subject say more than a few words. Indeed, out of the thirty-two shots in Grant's story,

Tuba speaks only in seven of them, three of which include the presence of Grant. On the other hand, in Ellick's story we can begin to see how the technique of cinéma vérité has been utilized to provide an intimate portrait of the family's day-to-day life on the brink of change. We see Mulala speak intimately about her father and the dangers involved. We see her getting ready for bed. We see her at prayer. We see her picking up and talking about her school uniform and how sad she is for not being able to wear it. These are the kinds of elements that define the differences in style between documentary journalism and conventional broadcast news.

To clearly illustrate the stylistic differences between the two, in the sequence of Grant's story where we hear Tuba speak: "I want to give peace to my country, to my nation, everyone" Grant follows with:

> The eleven-year-old is a self-styled warrior poet, a small girl pitting her pen against the Taliban's sword. A girl from a simple home in Islamabad, she says she is committed to truth. Through her words, she reflects the pain of other children in her country, the injustice of other girls denied an education, of schools burnt to the ground, books banned, and too much death.

This is followed by Tuba reciting a poem: "Tiny drops of tears. Their faces, like the angels, washed with their bloods. They sleep forever as with anger." That's Grant's sixty-seven words compared to Tuba's nineteen.

In contrast (again, realizing that Ellick and Ashraf are not seemingly on a length restriction, as Grant is), the filmmakers in the *New York Times* piece allow a girl outside a school to read an entire revolutionary letter against the Taliban, the only narration setting up what is to follow: "While boys' schools stay open, more than two hundred girls' schools have been blown up by the Taliban. At one of the remaining schools, a student who is veiled to protect her identity speaks out" (2:08–2:17). The student proceeds to read the letter for nearly a full minute (2:17–3:13), as Ellick cuts in scenes from around Swat valley, representing thematic visuals of the girl's argument. Ellick narrates for nine seconds, while she speaks for fifty-six seconds. See Figure 1.3.

While Grant provides punchy narration to move the story along (in essence, to create the story), Ellick and Sharaf approach their narration as a utilitarian need, providing just enough information for the viewer to understand the context of what they're about to see—opening the space for their characters to speak at length.

Of course the longer length of the project in the *New York Times* video helps when creating more depth. But these are the kinds of choices that online newspapers can offer—outside the corporate broadcast news model—allowing for the publication of a nearly fifteen-minute documentary that gets at the heart of what makes strong documentary journalism: a character-centered story of a man and his daughter standing up for their rights against the narrow spectrum of the Taliban's rule. We enter the world of the subject, the reporter mediating off screen through their shots and edits, providing us with the subject's voice in sincere visual moments, as if they're sharing a part of their life, rather than being used to illustrate a reporter's narration (which we see in Grant's CNN story).

While Ellick and Ashraf follow a traditional documentary mold, using an omniscient-voice narration to help contextualize their story, Dai Sugano's "Left Behind" (*San Jose Mercury News*, 2008) blows the doors off conventional forms of video journalism, and structures his work around a poetic style. See the video here: www.mercurynewsphoto.com/2008/leftbehind/.

Figure 1.3 A student reads a letter, a diatribe against the Taliban's edicts in "Class Dismissed in Swat Valley" (Courtesy *The New York Times*. ©2009 Used with permission.)

The rest of this book will explore and explain how you can engage in the documentary style in your own video journalism work.

WORKSHEET FOR DETERMINING THE STORY'S POTENTIAL FOR DOCUMENTARY WORK

These questions will help you think about whether or not you can shoot in a documentary style or if you should engage a TV news style for a particular story.

✧ Is it breaking news? If so, then go out and get the images and write the narration. Get the story done as quickly as possible. No time for documentary work.
✧ What's your deadline? If it's the same day, then TV news style may be the way to go. If you have more time, then you can develop a character-driven documentary-style piece.
✧ How much time can you spend with your character(s)? If you have a ten-minute interview and no time to "hang-out" with the character, then it's nearly impossible to develop a documentary piece. You need time to build up trust and create a connection with your primary character in order to develop the story into a documentary journalism piece. This may be a period of several hours or several days (sometimes more).
✧ Do you have the potential to shoot footage of the primary character doing actions—the means of showing them doing what they want?
✧ Can you collect audio to shape the tone of the work?

✧ Are the interviews compelling? The voice of the character(s) must be primary in shaping the story and the characters should be dynamic.

FOR FURTHER READING

Artis, Anthony. *The Shut Up and Shoot Documentary Guide*. Focal Press, 2007. For those who like to learn with pictures, Artis's book covers the basics of documentary production, including research and questions, as well as technical information, such as camera operation (and most of the tools of the camera, including white balance, iris control, shot sizes, and so on), how to record clean sound, set up lights, and more—all with color pictures. I recommend this book to every video journalism student just starting out and for print journalists who don't want to be intimidated by technology.

Rabiger, Michael. *Directing the Documentary*. Focal Press, 2009. The essential manual on documentary production. It'll likely have much more than you need, but reading the book and doing the exercises will be like taking two full semesters at a university film school. It not only includes the process of approaching documentary preproduction, production, and postproduction, but also the section on discovering your artistic voice is priceless—for it will help you define what your central concerns and themes are in life and how you can shape them in your docs.

Interlude

On Backpack Journalism—From an Interview with Video Journalist Bill Gentile, American University

BACKPACK JOURNALISM DEFINED

I define backpack journalism as [a] character-driven model done by one person who has got the luxury of time to spend with the subjects, to watch the subjects as the story evolves and change.

Backpack journalism is built more on the foundation of documentary photojournalism than it is on the 6 o'clock news. We don't do stand-ups and we normally don't do breaking news, because it just doesn't fit. Some of these models have certain things that they just work well with, and they have other things that they don't work well with. When I worked for Video News International, VNI, a company I went to work for in 1995, we did video journalism. We started out with the series, *Trauma: Life in the E.R.*, and we also did breaking news, and it evolved into people doing stand-ups and so forth, and that's what I refer to as video journalism. Backpack journalism is something different. Backpack journalism again is built on the foundation of documentary photojournalism. You go out and you spend weeks with these people, or at least days with them. You don't have a producer; you don't have a correspondent with perfect hair and perfect teeth.

CHARACTER-DRIVEN STORIES

The underlying premise of the backpack journalism methodology is that you can tell powerful stories more effectively through the prism of one person's experience. Or one platoon's experience, or one football team's experience, or one basketball team's experience. And from that experience viewers can extrapolate the reality of a larger phenomenon. And that's what we try to do, that's what we try to explain through one person's experience, or one character's—that's why we call them character-driven documentaries. . . .

VISUAL STORYTELLING

The underlying thesis is that the visual component of the model is the most powerful component. Why would you relinquish the most powerful component of the model to second-class citizenship by inserting a correspondent who's going to stand in front of a camera and tell you what the hell's going on? Why would you do that? It doesn't make sense.

I call it three-dimensional chess. You've got three components to this model. It's the visuals, and that's the engine inside the methodology. Then you have the natural sound on camera. It's what your subjects tell you, the cars passing by in the street; in the case of Afghanistan, it's the helicopters flying over and the guys firing machine guns. And then you've got your own narration, which connects the dots and tells you what all of this means.

A lot of what we see on television today, and much of what we see on the internet, reflects a real lack of understanding of the visual language. We've got too much of what they call spray and pray—put a wide-angle lens on a thing, blast everything in sight, and then pray to God that something is useable. That's not the way to do this kind of journalism. You have to understand the visual storytelling language to be able to practice this craft effectively.

You can use the shooting skills, the interviewing skills, to take them and be a video journalist to cover breaking news—that's fine. But I think part of what we're encountering now is a lack of understanding about [backpack journalism]: "How is this model applicable to this situation, and how is the other model applicable to that situation?" And this is going play out in the newsroom in discussions between the [video] practitioners and their managers or editors.

My greatest concern is that the fundamentals and the methodology will be used more often to save money than they will be to do effective visual storytelling.

When this model works, [such as with my piece] *Afghanistan: The Forgotten War* [www.pbs.org/now/shows/428/index.html], when this model works, it works. It rocks, it doesn't just work, it rocks. It's smokin'. But you can't apply this model to every situation. You simply can't. So it's up to the practitioners and the managers/producers to figure out, "What are the best practices?"

And that's another thing we're trying to do with this backpack journalism project at American University's School of Communication. . . . We're trying to say, "This is how you do it properly; don't do it this way because it's improper. These are the guys who're doing it right." We're trying to establish these best practices, not just for students, but for professionals in the field. And we're trying to give them the theoretical backup and background to be able to do this stuff right.

CHAPTER 2

Finding a Story and Shaping the Structure

Starting with Character in Jigar Mehta's "The Recession-Proof Artist"

INTRODUCTION TO CHARACTER AND STORY STRUCTURE

At the heart of every good story is a *character*. A story is not an issue. It is not an event. It is not a series of talking heads—people saying things. A good story may contain all of these elements, but a video journalism piece lacking a central character presented in a visually compelling way may cause viewers to lose interest. *Character and story structure* mean the story is character-centered, not issue-focused. The voice of the subject comes through strongly, providing a central character who wants or needs something. This need or want induces dramatic action and tends to provide the story structure. Any larger issues, if any, come from the subject, who may be used as a case study of an issue—a character by which the issue is embodied. Breaking news or issue-oriented stories do not necessarily engage in character-centered stories.

In this chapter, I examine character and story structure in Jigar Mehta's "The Recession-Proof Artist" produced for the *New York Times*. It includes screen grabs from the first second of each shot, placed within a classic story structure model. Although I will examine some of the elements of cinematography and editing—and these must be mentioned since it's difficult to separate character and story structure from the visual cinematic elements—the primary focus will be on story structure as it relates to character.

Tip: Travis Fox on Character

I don't mean to say that I start off with characters and figure out what the story is. You figure out what the story is and in order to tell that story, you find characters and visually interesting scenes. For longer pieces, you deal with character development. It's almost like a feature-film way of looking at it. Your character has a conflict or has to overcome something and changes in the meantime. There's some overlap with Hollywood—this is what quality video storytelling is (Pitzer 2010).

Character and Dramatic Structure

Characters drive dramatic structure. Philosopher Aristotle, in his observation of ancient Greek plays, saw certain patterns in playwrights' dramatic structures, and his work, *Poetics*, is an outline of his notes that have influenced narratives in the West. Although dealing strictly with fictional stage plays, some of his notes are useful for video journalists who want to up their storytelling game. "Character is that which reveals moral purpose," Aristotle says, "showing what kind of things a [person] chooses or avoids. Speeches [or stories], therefore, which do not make this manifest, or in which the [character] does not choose or avoid anything whatever, are not expressive of character" (Aristotle n.d.).

Aristotle further defines action as the central condition of all good Greek drama. These actions are caused by characters

> who necessarily possess certain distinctive qualities both of character and thought; for it is by these that we qualify actions themselves, and these—thought and character—are the two natural causes from which actions spring, and on actions again all success or failure depends. Hence, the Plot is the imitation of the action— for by plot I here mean the arrangement of the incidents.

Here are two major principles that video journalists can follow when choosing and creating their stories. A character must want something, for if a character is static, not choosing or avoiding anything, then there's nobody to propel the story forward—there is no dramatic need for an audience to gain emotional attachment and they'll move on and find a story that does. And secondly, these actions, the plot elements revealing the dramatic needs of the character, must be arranged in a way that structures and builds emotional attachment successfully.

The typical story structure follows this pattern:

- hook, followed by the introduction or setup (Act 1)
- conflict or complications (rising action) (Act 2)
- climax (or the crisis point) and resolution (Act 3).

A hook is some incident that grabs the audience's attention right away. We're provided some kind of background or context or introduction to the character or situation. There's some obstacle the character must overcome, or a question that needs to get answered. In order to get what she wants, this conflict builds to a climax where the character either gets what she wants or doesn't. Finally, the resolution reveals what the character learnt from her experience. The dramatic structure typically falls on a time-intensity graph, first formulated by the German playwright and novelist Gustav Freytag in his 1863 work *The Technique of Drama*. The basic structure is used in playwriting and screenplay writing texts. See Figure 2.1.

Characters have a need, typically in conflict with something or somebody, and they attempt to fulfill that need, overcoming obstacles and learning something about themselves in the process. Characters *do* and this doing drives the plot—the arrangement of actions. All good video journalism has at its core some element of this character need and story structure. Since video journalism is a visual and aural medium, stories that reveal characters and their needs visually and aurally tend to make for stronger video journalism. I don't think an audience wants to be *told* what a character wants—they prefer to *see* their natural behavior as they attempt to get what they want.

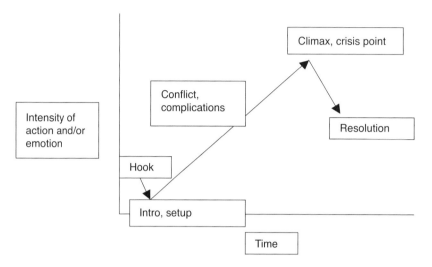

Figure 2.1 Classic Story Structure, Building in Emotional Intensity over Time.

Tip: Learn How to Tell a Good Story by Jigar Mehta

If you learn these classic [story] structures that work for a reason, and you're able to tell the stories in those ways, I think that's good. That's key. And I think people see that you do good work, and you'll get a job. I was watching last night *This American Life* on Showtime, about this Iraqi American, what he does is, and I think that they kind of pushed him to do this gimmicky thing that I would never do, but, they made him set up a stand that says, "Talk to an Iraqi." And, you know they had people come up and interact with him. It made me think about ways to tell stories. I always like to see what other people are doing out there, and I think a lot of times people don't look enough at what their colleagues are doing. And that's my other advice, inundate yourself with what other people out there are doing, because you might get a little something that might help improve your storytelling.

Tip: Embody the Points You Want to Make through Character. Bill Gentile, American University

Bill Gentile is a practicing video journalist who engages in solo-shooting "backpack journalism" style. He teaches at American University in Washington, D.C. He conducts workshops in the field and his work can be found at his website: www.billgentile.com.

I did a piece called *Nurses Needed* about the nursing shortage in the United States for *PBS Now*. I started out with a pile of documents about six inches high—newspaper articles, official

US Government statistics, magazine pieces, foundation studies—and I understood from the beginning the editorial points that we have to make. But my approach was to not just get people to tell me this to camera, not have the correspondent say this and use the video as a backdrop.

"My approach was [to] find the characters who embody these points that we want to make. And that's the way we approached the piece. And at the end of the year, that piece was named [. . .] the number one most popular piece of all of 2008. [. . .] The *Afghanistan* piece was named number three. So for the whole year I had the number one, and the number three most popular pieces that *Now* broadcast in 2008. And it was not because I'm brilliant—because I'm not—but because I used the methodology properly, and we found those characters who embodied the points that we wanted to make. [We didn't have the host] David Brancaccio come in, interview people, make his points, and have the video used as wallpaper behind it. We didn't do that. We imposed the backpack documentary, or the backpack journalism model, and it worked. Brilliantly."

Nurses Needed is located at: www.pbs.org/now/shows/442/index.html.

HOW TO DEVELOP A STORY—ASK KEY QUESTIONS BEFORE YOU START SHOOTING

As you go out and find stories, remember, not every story needs to be shot on video. Many will work just fine as a written story in print or online. However, if what you come across excites you visually—compelling images worth thousands of words—then pull out the camera and start shooting. But be sure what you're shooting is tied to a central character. There needs to be a story tied to these images and characters are the best way storytellers use to convey their stories.

Before you begin shooting, answer these questions:

- Who is your character and what makes him or her tick? You need to get personal.
- What is the story in one sentence? Be sure the summary contains the seed of a conflict. I can summarize, for example, Eliot Rausch's "The Last Minutes with Oden" (http://vimeo.com/8191217): A man in prison for ten years discovers how to love unconditionally from his dog, but has to put him down.
- A summary of the story. Identify the possible hook, conflict, climax, and resolution.
- What are some of the possible actions you can get on camera? (The visual material.) How will the shots in each sequence show the hook, conflict, climax, and resolution?

Tip: Pre-interview Your Subject by Jigar Mehta

I pre-interview folks as much as possible when the opportunity arises. For example with Alex, I had a good half-hour- or hour-long conversation. I'll ask very open-ended questions just to see if they can fill in the void. Rather than a yes-no question, and seeing how they respond to yes-no questions, the open-ended questions don't make or break a character, but they're a very good tell—so I can tell if I can do a sit-down interview with them to help them guide the story, or if I'm going to have to have the piece be more narration driven.

- Why must this story be told and why must you do it? Why should the audience care? (In other words, tell me how the story is compelling and why it's important that you tell this story. Shape the story around a universal theme by which an audience can identify, such as a "Living within your means" in "The Recession-Proof Artist.")

As you answer these questions, the story will begin to fall into place. The rest of it is up to your talent as a shooter and thinking through the shots cinematically. But first and foremost is character.

CASE STUDY—"THE RECESSION-PROOF ARTIST" BY JIGAR MEHTA (47 SHOTS, 4:15), THE *NEW YORK TIMES* (2009)

http://video.nytimes.com/video/2009/05/19/arts/1194840314497/the-recession-proof-artist.html

Jigar Mehta's documentary journalism piece provides a simple example of how a visually powerful work can be created when the video journalist engages—whether consciously or unconsciously—character-structured storytelling. It's not breaking-news, a political analysis, or an unraveling of a crisis, but this example reflects the core themes of Aristotle, making it a strong work of documentary journalism.

In examining the character, Mehta gives voice to his subject—to Alexander Conner—a student just out of university, living on a $12,000 annual budget as he pursues his dream of making it as an artist in Philadelphia. No narration provided by a reporter. No heavy-handed production telling the audience how to think or feel. Just Conner's voice telling it as he sees it.

By focusing on character, Mehta takes us into the personal life-space of Conner. Many documentary filmmakers build trust and take us into a slice of life of their characters. We see Conner create art on his living room floor, make bread in his kitchen, and smoke as he talks about how he gets by on $12,000 per year. Because the documentary journalist respects Conner, we sense that he respects Mehta by opening up to Mehta's lens, and for this, we the audience, get to share those personal moments by putting us in Conner's living room. And this is one of the core differences between broadcast news and documentary filmmaking—the building of that trust in order to get the subject to open up and share their personal lives.

"The Recession-Proof Artist" began as solicitations on the *New York Times* "Art Beats" blog. Mehta says that a reporter, Robin Pogrebin, screened a dozen different people until she found Conner in Philadelphia. Mehta knew he had potential as a character, because "he was able to tell this larger story about how to be a recession-proof artist. He had those aspects of being young and hungry, that he was on this trajectory of being an artist for life." Mehta didn't want just anyone, the successful artist being shown at galleries, "adjusting what they do because of the recession," he says. With Conner, Mehta explains that "even if times are gangbusters, he'd still be making bread, he'd still be living paycheck to paycheck. So, that's where I came up with the title, 'The Recession-Proof Artist.'"

Having studied documentary techniques under the tutelage of documentary filmmaker Jon Else at UC Berkeley's School of Journalism, Mehta has learned to make a connection with his subject before pulling out the camera.

> I went to Philadelphia around noon. Alex Conner had finished work, and was hanging out at home, and for the first hour and a half we just chatted. Like talking about the neighborhood, talking about his art, just getting a sense of who he is. And a lot of this is just [to build rapport]. A lot of this is just letting them get comfortable with you, right? And [you're approaching it] like, "Okay, who is this guy?" We get to know the person, just having a good time, and then at a certain point you start talking about, "Okay well where are some things that we can start filming?" "Where are you going to be?" With Alex, it was like, "Well do you want to do some art today?"

This allows the journalist to get a sense of the story, the dramatic structure, as based on the needs and wants of the character. Mehta discovered how Conner's dramatic need is tied to the emotional need to do his art—and within this need lies the roots of conflict: he'll do his art even if that means working in a museum for low pay, using his money to buy art supplies, and drawing on his living room floor as the largest space he has to do his art. In this story, his emotional desire is never fully realized. We're looking at a moment of time where Conner's life-stage is still in flux, where we can see his conflict, how he copes with his desire, and how he rationalizes his lifestyle. It's real life in an unresolved state.

Shaping Character through Cinematography

I'll cover cinematography in more detail in the next chapter, but I wanted to point out how Mehta uses his lens in a cinematic way in order to embody and show his character *doing something*. Characters do actions and, although we see Conner sitting in an interview, it is used sparingly by Mehta. Rather than shoot to script—with shots found to illustrate a story—as sometimes produced in broadcast journalism, Mehta shoots like a photographer—a cinematographer, one who knows how to use light and shadow to reveal a character's emotional core. He was able to get these intimate shots by "knowing how to interact with subjects," he says, "knowing that I can be an inch away from him, and part of that process is something I learned when I worked on my first documentary, *My Flesh and Blood*." As one of the shooters on the project, where he helped shoot a large family with disabilities, Mehta

> learned very quickly that the closer you get to your subject—once you've developed that relationship with them—and then you get the camera out and you get in their face, and get them comfortable with it, the sooner they forget about it, and then the really good stuff starts to happen because they become less conscious of the camera. With kids they just get bored with the camera because it doesn't do anything after a while.

We can see the strength of Mehta's cinematography just in the first five shots, covering the first thirty-five seconds of the piece. The shots reveal strong composition and lighting. See shots 1–5, pp. 24 and 25.

In the first shot, the background wall is lit, but Conner's foreground is dark, with back light washing over his right arm as he draws—the light catching the pen and hitting the paper, drawing our focus to his work. A cup foregrounds the composition. Notice there is no wide "establishing shot," another weak point found in too much of broadcast news. The medium-length lens allows for sharp focus on Conner, but a soft focus on the cup and background wall—we can see what these objects are, they provide atmosphere, but our main focus is on Conner doing his art. We see the character *doing*—expressing his core desire of being an artist. We're not being spoon-fed through a reporter's narration, such as: "Conner struggles as an artist in his tiny apartment where he must draw on the floor in order to create his art." That's a reporter telling the audience what they're seeing. By using the shots to tell the story, rather than with narration, Mehta allows the audience to enter the story at the subject's own pace, to draw their own conclusions, and to feel the emotion contained in the shot, rather than having the reporter tell us how to feel.

The second shot reveals a strong diagonal, pointing the viewer to Conner's drawing, highlighting his work process. In *The Visual Story: Creating the Visual Structure of Film, TV, and Digital Media* (Focal Press, 2008), Bruce Block provides an overview of the visual components—space, line and shape, tone, color, movement, and rhythm—used to tell stories visually. In the section on line and shape, Block contends: "The diagonal line is the most intense, the vertical line is less intense, and the horizontal line is the least dynamic or intense line" (p. 101). The high-angle diagonal draws our energy down to Conner's art, an act of visual storytelling that compels our attention to the action.

In the third, we see a wider shot, revealing his tight work space as Conner draws cramped on the floor, pieces of art scattered, Mehta using part of the sofa or bed in the foreground, giving the shot a sense of depth. Notice the strong diagonal of light and shadow on the back wall. This backlighting also provides a sense of depth in the two-dimensional frame. Mehta does not use this as the opening shot, establishing Conner's space, because the story isn't about the space—it's about Conner doing his art, so the opening shot puts us into Conner's world, his art-making, and Mehta's composition and sense of lighting hooks us, and we want to see more. Also note that the art Conner draws is different from the one in shot 2. At first glance we probably don't notice, and neither do we care, because Mehta draws us into the emotional core of the scene and, since the shots are edited for emotion, we tend not to notice the visual incongruity.

The fourth shot is similar to shot 1, but notice the light and focus present a different story. We can see him at work, but the focus in the background is now sharp, allowing us to see what the photos on the wall are, as well as his bed. We're now seeing the conflict Conner is in: he's not doing his art in a studio—we're in his living-space. He's willing to struggle to do his art, to do what he loves. The shot reveals conflict and heightens the dramatic tension. The light falls on his blue pen and arms, his face washed in a soft fill light—he is not bothered by his circumstances. He is focused and we get the sense of joy in his expression.

And in the fifth shot of the opening sequence we get a standard head shot, but slightly askew, Mehta giving us a slight diagonal to increase energy. This shot does indeed reveal Conner's satisfaction in his life. We also see other art on the wall, the background and foreground in focus allowing us to see even more of his personal space.

When shooting, Mehta says he approaches his work like a photographer.

> Some of the shots I was tucked in behind his desk, underneath a chair, and just waiting for him to come into frame and come out of frame. And, when he missed—not his fault, he's just doing what he's doing—I missed, I was able to readjust, and get it the second

time as he came in to do something. There's going to be repetitive motions—this is not something he's doing within five minutes. Over the course of that night, he spent six hours on his art. The [final edit] might've been out of sequence, but it's not about [showing him] making this one piece. It's about the idea that he makes this art in one room. And so that's what I was trying to get across.

Mehta chose to begin Conner's narration in shot 2, propelling it through the shot. Most of the speech is informational and, if there's a weakness to this film, it lies in the fact that Mehta didn't have the time or take the time to show Conner in his work environment, and this is one of the key differences between documentary film and video journalism—time. In documentaries, the filmmaker may spend months with a subject, providing a profile of different moments from their life, while the video journalist will typically spend a day or part of a day with their subject. So when Conner talks about how one of his joys is to go to a local shop to get an apple fritter and a cup of coffee on pay day, we don't see this—it is told to us by Conner. The film would be more powerful with that scene in it. Mehta discusses how he wanted to go in with some story ideas, such as "I should probably go with him to work, I should probably go with him around Philadelphia as he tries to sell his art, or display his art, or he's going to have meetings about setting up a gallery." However, after hanging out with Conner, Mehta realized that it was more "appropriate to contain it within his personal space." The piece became an intimate portrait of an artist trying to make it.

Tip: Spending Time with Your Subject by Jigar Mehta

When shooting, I don't go in with preconceived ideas. I have a mental list of things that would be great to get, but my sort of filmmaking is about being honest and being about whatever you are going to do, I am going to film you doing. I don't want to say, "Oh I missed that shot of you making that or the way you put the pen to the paper there, and then moved around because you were thinking about something. Could you just do that again, because I really missed it?" I [observe], "Okay, that's a trait that he has," and I'll just position myself, and it's almost like nature photography.

When you spend more and more time with folks you start to notice they have little traits, and those are very telling traits. People point out how "The Recession-Proof Artist" is such a telling piece about Conner's personality, it was the way he lit cigarettes, for example. He was mimicking [behavior]—he learned it from somewhere else, like he's straight out of Central Casting [of] this young artist [who lights cigarettes]. And so I [noticed], "Oh that's kind of cool how he was doing it," and he was smoking a lot, and so it wasn't like that was the only cigarette he lit, so I knew that I wanted to get that shot. When he was about to light up, I just prepared for it and got the shot.

I never stage anything. If my shots are not perfect or if they're sloppy that's just because that's the way it is. If I miss something, I just missed it. But it's also like the agreement I've made with the audience. It's like the audience knows at the end of the piece—they get out of it everything I put in front of them. It's not like I withheld a piece of information from them. I'm all about full disclosure.

Below are the forty-seven shots that comprise this 4:15 second piece. From this list I will identify the dramatic structure within the work. The shot order goes from left to right, top to bottom.

The opening four shots comprise the hook to the story—the emotional power contained in the cinematography of these shots help pull the viewer into it.

Hook—Shots 1–4 (0:00–0:33)

Conner provides narration starting in shot 2, which also leads us into the exposition—the context for the story, the information needed for the audience to understand what's going on. Beginning on shot 2, we hear him say:

> For God's sake, I've only been out of university not even a year. I don't understand why in the world I should expect to have things roll around my way. I've had a lot of friends who have been very upset by the fact that they've only been out not yet a year and they haven't broken—Charles Saatchi hasn't come knocking at their door.

The shots combined with this quote sets up the theme and conflict of Mehta's video story. Note, as Conner talks, we can hear his pen scraping on paper, and in the fourth shot we see him talking as he draws. The natural sound adds to the emotional depth of the story, since we're being put into his space visually and aurally. Getting clean natural audio is as important— and often more important—than getting strong video. Without clean audio, no one will "see"

1

2

3

4

the video. In addition, Mehta chose to open the piece with light-hearted music that provides an uplifting emotional tone to the work.

Tip: Starting and Ending the Piece by Jigar Mehta

Getting a film started and getting a film landed, are the two most difficult things. The middle's the easy part. And you always see, especially at film festivals, whenever you walk out of there, you go like, "Man, that was like ten minutes too long," and it's just because they didn't quite land it right, or the take-off wasn't quite there, and so I think if you can nail those two bits down—starting the piece and landing it—the middle to me is fairly easy, because you're just getting across information at that point.

Did I get the beginning? Did I get the end shot? I thought maybe I would start with a slap of the bread on the pan, because I had a shot of that, and then I thought maybe I'd start with him, just various shots of him—before you'd reveal his face, like him just doing this, and him smoking, and then you see he's like this 22-year old kid in a kind of run-down part of Philadelphia.

Introduction/Setup—Shots 5–7 (0:34–1:02)

The exposition provides the information needed to follow the main thrust of the story. It sets up who the character is and their central concern.

5

6

7

The shots include Conner talking in a formal interview, as well as his voice underlying his working on art:

> My name is Alexander Conner. I'm twenty-two years old. I live in Philadelphia. I make about $12,000 a year and I'm an artist. I work at the Philadelphia Museum of Art in two departments. I work in the telemarketing department as well as education, working with students in the student center. That's about thirty-six hours a week. I end up being able to spend the rest of the time keeping my head in the art.

We get the sense of who he is and we also receive the seeds to the central conflict—a low-paying job at an art museum. A young man attempting to live his dream while keeping his feet in the arts. During his free time he works on this art. And despite the fact we don't see Conner in his workplace environment—which we might see in a long-form documentary—the exposition he does provide acts as a kind of contrapuntal moment. This is an aural and visual montage where an unrelated element—narration—and the visual—Conner working on his art—create the idea of a struggling artist, and the seeds of the conflict.

Conflict/Complications—Shots 8–25 (1:03–2:48)

The conflict comprises the core of the drama—it's the stuff that makes an audience stay tuned to the work, because they want to see how a person overcomes a problem—and it, perhaps, becomes the means by which they can assess their own lives and their own conflicts, and learn lessons by which another person struggles to overcome, providing them with hope.

Shots 8–16 Conflict/Complication 1

As Conner speaks, we hear about how he lives on a small budget and still maintains his art: "I work only to kind of sustain my ability to make my own art and pay my bills. So I make a grand a month. So $475 of that is to rent. $75 of that is to utilities. $200 of that is to savings. $50–75 is to food. And the [rest] is the money to buy supplies, get film processed, and whatever else I need." We see him work at his art, as well as a shot showing a cupboard with V8 juices and ramen noodles (shot 11)—the food of a "starving artist." Some of his art supplies come from paper and material thrown away at the museum where he works.

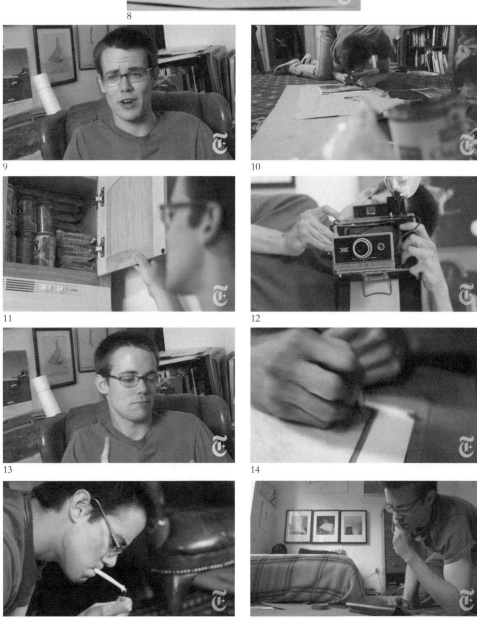

Shots 8–16 Conflict/Complication 1 . . . *continued*

Shots 17–22 Conflict/Complication 2

The conflict intensifies as Conner discusses making some basic bread, "because I ran out of money from my last paycheck, and payday isn't until Thursday. It's just going to be flower, baking soda, and yeast" (17–22). This is a powerful human moment, showing Conner upbeat as he discusses how he stretches his budget, paycheck to paycheck.

Shots 17–22 Conflict/Complication 2

Shots 23–25 Conflict/Complication 3

The scene is followed by him smoking (23–25), further propelling the conflict, for now we see him extend his budget to an unnecessary extravagance: "This is basically my big confusing the concept of a want with a need. I . . . don't need to smoke"—we hear his pause and we can feel his internal struggle as he rationalizes his desire. "If you ask me, I would tell you I needed to, but really I want to. I could quit, theoretically." Here, again, we see an honest human moment come through, we sense sincerity, and it is in conflict of his overall need—to create art.

23

24

25

Shots 23–25 Conflict/Complication 3

Climax/crisis point—Shots 26–37 (2:49–3:40)

The next sequence encompasses the climax, revealing shots of his art for the first time, releasing us from the tension about what the audience has been wondering—what does Conner's art look like? Is it any good?

Shots 26–31 Climax

Mehta holds back, revealing Conner's art for the climactic moment. Since the beginning of the year, he has created fifty prints and drawings, as well as well as four to five hundred photographs. We then hear Conner's heart-felt expression, revealed during his close-up interview: "I have to make. If I couldn't, what else would I do? And I'm a very good artist."

26

27

continued overleaf . . .

Shots 26–31 Climax . . . *continued*

Shots 32–37 Climax Continued

The remaining shots of the climax (32–37), reveal how he is able to be the "recession-proof artist" that Mehta claims him to be. The shots reveal where he works, explains how he draws on cardboard, and states "How I was very blessed. After graduating college, I have no student debt. My parents were kind enough to be able to pay for it. If I did, this would not be a game plan that I could really work with." The climax gives us the peak of the conflict and reveals how he overcomes his core need.

continued overleaf . . .

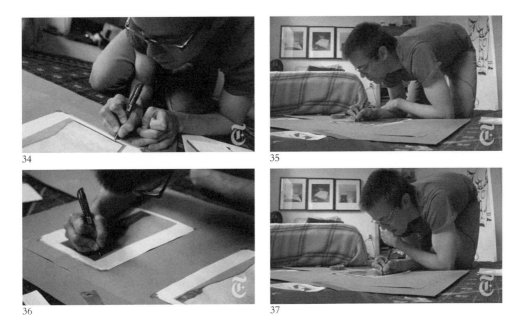

Shots 32–37 Climax Continued . . . *continued*

Resolution—Shots 38–47 (3:41–4:15)

The resolution takes us back to the beginning (38–47), Mehta showing Conner working on his art. Music picks up, again, as we see shot 38—one of my favorites—revealing the only long shot in the piece: Conner down a hall and through a doorway.

continued overleaf . . .

42   43
44   45
46   47

Shots 38–47 Resolution . . . *continued*

We hear Conner speak over these shots:

> It's between buying paint and buying dinner. If you're not one of those kinds of people, you won't kind of survive. It's good that those people will not be out in the market-place as much. It just won't be a viable career opportunity. My five-year plan? Yeah, I would like to sustainably be making my art. If I could achieve that—which is a huge achievement—to be able to support yourself on your own work, that would be wonderful.

Here we may not get the resolution of Conner's life and art, but we do get the sense of his plan and his final wish of being able to support himself with his art within five years.

In summary, then, we can chart the dramatic structure of Mehta's video journalism piece on Figure 2.2.

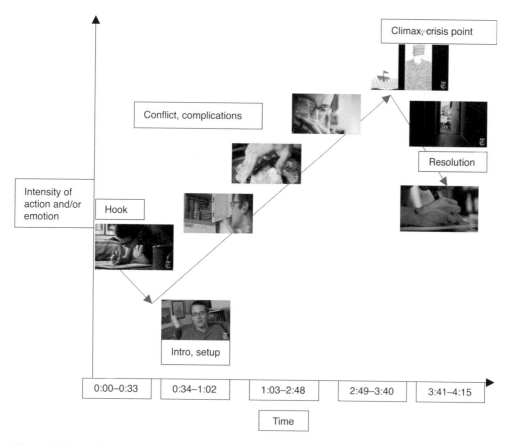

Figure 2.2 Story Graph.

Mehta is an artist, portraying an artist in his personal space, allowing the artist to speak his mind, and does so in a visually compelling way.

WORKSHEET EXERCISE—INTERVIEW A STRANGER

Talk to somebody you do not know. Do not bring a camera. Just talk to them. You need to develop an honesty and intimacy similar to how you might perform on a date. Be honest and open, and, as you build trust in the conversation, begin to ask personal questions. Discover a story or two that's unique to them. After the interview, write it down in a journal.

Take one of the stories and identify the need of the main character. What do they want or need? What did they do to get what they wanted?

Next, take one of the stories and map it out on a story arc: hook or inciting incident, introduction or exposition, conflict or complications that build to a climax, followed by some kind of resolution. Write one-sentence summaries of the story elements and put it on a story graph.

Write out any possible visual actions and place them with the story summaries on the story graph. Share the story in class.

WORKSHEET FOR CHARACTER AND STORY DEVELOPMENT

As you do research on your story and conduct pre-interviews, answer the following questions as a way to determine the potential of a character in relationship to story structure.

- ✧ What does the character want? This is the core of the dramatic action. If this is an issue-based story, then find out how the character embodies the issue.
- ✧ What actions does the character take to try and achieve it? This needs to be visual, because characters must do something.
- ✧ What prevents the character from getting it? This is the conflict, the complications the character faces in attempting to achieve their goal.
- ✧ What does the character learn from the experience, whether they're successful or not? This will help map the resolution.

Sketch out your answers on the story chart, by answering the following questions:

- ✧ What is the possible hook?
- ✧ What is the possible set-up?
- ✧ What are some potential complications, or elements of conflict?
- ✧ What is the crisis point, the climactic moment of the story?
- ✧ What is the resolution?

Can you identify the decisive moment for each of these? What might they be?

FOR FURTHER READING

Bernard, Sheila. *Documentary Storytelling*. Focal Press, 2007. Great book on providing the basics of storytelling foundation. Includes interviews with documentary film-makers.

Mamet, David. *On Directing Film*. Penguin, 1992. Yes, it's a book on fiction filmmaking, but Mamet—being the Pulitzer Prize-winning playwright that he is—clarifies the logic of storytelling shot by shot. Espousing a visual approach, Mamet takes care to explain the process by which the dramatic structure grows from the central theme or idea, plays through a sequence, the scene, and on down to the shot. Anything extraneous to the character's need should be dropped from the film. Documentary journalists focusing on characters will find his notes useful. It includes a transcript of Mamet interacting with students in a film class at Columbia University. The short read is worth checking out.

Rabiger, Michael. *Developing Story Ideas*. Focal Press, 2005. Rabiger provides dozens of exercises designed to help readers discover their strengths and weaknesses as storytellers. Some of the best work coming from documentary storytellers derives from their own personal life experiences as they tap into these personal themes in order to help discover characters and stories that mean something to them. A lot of exercises to help you find your voice and tap into your creative potential. Also includes fantastic tools on how to analyze story structure.

Interlude

Becoming a Documentary Journalist—From an Interview with the Renaud Brothers[3]

The illustrious *American Cinematographer* says this about the Renaud Brothers: "The cinema verite label often is misapplied in the film industry, but on the Renauds the tag sticks, reinforcing the notion that content is king" (Renaud Brothers, 2011).

The award-winning filmmakers' work includes: *Warrior Champions*, *Little Rock Central: 50 Years Later*, *Taking the Hill*, *Off to War*, and *Dope Sick Love*. Their most recent work, "The Heroes of Children's Hospital," aired on NBC's Dateline on January 31, 2010.

They also produce short docs for the *New York Times*, which have included forays into Juarez, and most recently a trip to Haiti, following the devastating earthquake in 2010. The interview below was conducted via email after their return from Haiti, and it reveals some of their secrets wedding the vision of documentary journalism and documentary filmmaking.

BECOME AN EDITOR FIRST

We both started our career working for the documentary filmmaker and former *NBC News* correspondent Jon Alpert (*Life of Crime*, *Baghdad ER*, *Alive Day Memories*). From him we learned a lot about the craft, but also about surviving and thriving and coming back with the story in some of the most dangerous places in the world. We started out as editors as I believe all young filmmakers should do. If you can become a good editor first, it is easy to become a good shooter.

PRODUCING VIDEO FOR THE *NEW YORK TIMES*

At a time when television news invests less and less in foreign stories, the *New York Times* has stepped up in a serious way and is leading the field online in producing original foreign news video content for the web. Dave Rummel and Ann Derry at the *Times* are both veterans of television news and documentary, and among the best producers we have worked with.

This kind of reporting is expensive and requires a lot of resources and the fact that the *Times* put people like Dave and Ann in place to head up the division shows the commitment they have to the form. We worked a lot with the excellent *Discovery/Times* channel when it was broadcasting, and it has been a natural fit for us to work at NYtimes.com.

In producing stories, we work together with Dave Rummel in a way that is very similar to that in the television world. We submit a rough cut of our stories and the producers give us notes and it's a back and forth collaboration. What makes publishing online different is that a story can be "broadcast" twenty-four hours a day seven days a week, whenever news is happening, from anywhere in the world. We love that excitement and freedom, but there are challenges. Filing stories from a disaster or war zone can be difficult. Sometimes, as was the case in Haiti, the only means of transmitting our stories is by a portable BGAN satellite system. This is expensive, and the file sizes have to be small. Often there is only one opportunity to send the story, and back and forth editing with a producer in NY is impossible. So being on the same page with the producers on the front end is important. We trust them and they trust us. The best supervising producers are the ones who don't have an ego in the fight. In other words their only interest in altering a story is to make it better. With Dave we know that when he gets involved in shaping a story, the work will only improve.

SAVING LIVES ON THE *USNS COMFORT*

Haiti had been out of the news for a while when we requested the *Times* send us there in November. It seems ironic now, but we wanted to go there to report on the ways in which this country with so tragic a history seemed to be turning a corner. Over the last forty years, Haiti has experienced one disaster after another—the AIDS epidemic, political coups, foreign occupations and embargoes, and serious criminal gang activity that has paralyzed the country, preventing foreign investment and the development of a tourism industry to match its neighbors in the rest of the Caribbean. Most people were not aware of the fact, however, that in 2009 the security situation with the help of a UN peacekeeping force was under control, many of the gang leaders were in jail, and the political environment was relatively stable. UN Envoy Bill Clinton was actively promoting foreign investment, new roads and airports were in the planning stages. This was the kind of underreported story we like and think is important, and the *Times* agreed to let us report on it. And then, shortly after we returned to the States the earthquake hit, and we knew we had to go back, if nothing else than to update the stories we had just shot, and find out what happened to the Haitian people we had met there. (See the video at http://vimeo.com/9232982.)

CHARACTER

In our long-form documentary work everything is about character. We are more likely to start a project with a character we like rather than an issue or a story. The short-form news stories that we produce for the *Times* are a little different, but not a lot. With these stories often we are starting from a larger concept, like the Drug War in Juarez, or the earthquake in Haiti, but whereas most news stories are dominated by a correspondent either on camera or in voice-over, we are still looking for characters to drive the story. We do use some voice-over in these news pieces because it helps focus and keep the stories short. However, we use as little as possible. We believe the look on a child's face, or a gesture from a politician, uncommented can sometimes speak worlds more than an all knowing voice-over.

Both of us shoot, produce, and edit. We are totally interchangeable and you would never know which of us is behind the camera. This allows us to cover a lot of ground at once, multiple characters and story lines.

NARRATION

Most TV news pieces are edited like radio. This is how reporters turn them around so fast. In fact they often call the first pass of a story a radio cut. We learnt to make documentaries first, and are still learning about making news stories. We still like to rely on the footage and our characters first, and we write the narration around that. Usually for us the narration is not even so much necessary as it is often repeating what is already said in the story, but by saying it in narration helps us shorten the piece to the appropriate lengths.

GETTING ACCESS

We are used to working with the military, having been embedded for long periods of time in Iraq and having worked with the US Paralympic Military program on a recent project. We were given exclusive documentary access to the *USNS Comfort* on this trip. We were able to go wherever we wanted any time we wanted on the ship. This kind of work is our specialty; we know how to get as close as you possibly can and still not disrupt the process. You have to get close, but you can't get kicked out. It's a delicate balance. The military no doubt wants press for a mission like this with the *USNS Comfort* hospital ship—it's a humanitarian mission that paints them in a good light. So we understand that. We just always try to use the access we are given in a way to tell a unique human interest story that brings something new to a larger news story.

"WE DON'T GET OVERWHELMED"

We have spent the last decade working in the toughest parts of the world. Like an ER doctor you get accustomed to the suffering, keeping in perspective that what you are doing is for a greater good. I think we were just born to do this. We don't get overwhelmed, fear never paralyzes us, and we are able to work through just about anything. This is our job. I don't think we are adrenaline junkies like some of the war correspondents we know. We don't seek *out* the dangerous assignments. But once we are committed to a story, we are willing to do whatever it takes to tell that story.

FINDING THE CHARACTER

We are always looking for characters who we believe provide a unique window into a news story. And of course the access those characters can give you is crucial. In one of our stories for the *New York Times* we met Alix Sainvil, a Haitian American UN cop who was working inside Cité Soleil, one of the most dangerous slums in the world. What better way to see what is going on there than through the eyes of someone who American audiences can relate to, but who is Haitian and knows the forbidding streets of Cité Soleil as well as anybody? On top of that, he is an emotional, thinking man; he speaks from the heart and not like a spokesperson. That is gold.

SECURITY IN AN INSECURE LAND

In covering the drug wars in Juarez, we focused on the children who have been affected by it most. In particular a boy whose father was a hitman for one of the cartels and was murdered. When you tell audiences that Juarez is the most dangerous city in the world with executions on the streets in broad daylight common, it is hard for an audience to wrap their heads around that, to really feel what that is like and what it means. But profile a child who is articulate, genuine, and it puts a human face on the issue that audiences can relate to.

TELLING THE STORIES THAT DON'T GET TOLD

We love to tell stories that won't get told otherwise or at least not in the same way. In one story we produced for the *New York Times* recently, we focused on the young Haitian American Navy Corpsmen aboard the *USNS Comfort* hospital ship who have been called upon to be translators for victims of the earthquake in Haiti. With no training at all, these young men and women stepped up and became a lifeline for vulnerable Haitian patients coming aboard the ship, a foreign country really, unfamiliar and scary. The Corpsmen comfort the patients and attend to their needs, letting them know that the United States is here to help. Sometimes they tell the patients that their legs will be amputated, or even that they will soon die. Through the experience of these translators the viewer is given a totally different and interesting look at this crisis. These Corpsmen are national heroes, and had we not profiled them, very few people would have known it. Showing things like this to the world is something that makes us proud.

Whatever the sacrifices, any time we get to do this kind of work and be a part of history as it unfolds, it's worth it. There are fewer and fewer places where this kind of work can get seen. The *New York Times* is one of the places picking up the slack right now, and we hope that they can succeed in this mission.

CHAPTER 3

Shooting the Image

Composition and Lighting in Travis Fox's "Narcocorridos and Nightlife in Mexicali" and "Crisis in Darfur Expands"

INTRODUCTION TO COMPOSITION AND LIGHTING

A video story is different from a print story in the type of vocabulary used. In a print story, journalists obviously craft stories from words made up of visual symbols of the alphabet in order to shape meaning—they're culturally and socially learned. Most of us learn grammar in grade school and are given reading and writing exercises to build vocabulary and to learn how to write. However, even though we're exposed to more visual media today than in any other period of human history—from watching television, films, and media on the internet—most of us are not taught how to read and write visually, cinematically. Our media literacy lags behind our textual literacy.

A basic vocabulary of how to read and write cinematically must be learnt before we can become better video journalists. Most of us can't watch a good video and just pick up the skills to shoot good stuff through osmosis. We need to take the time to master how the video journalist utilizes the cinematic palette before we can learn how to make the best choices in the creation of video documentaries. Just as a writer chooses certain words to engage emotions, provide information, and structure them to tell a story, the video journalist must engage elements of a cinema vocabulary—comprised of shot sizes, composition, camera movement, lighting, sound, and pacing through editing—in order to tell a story visually. This chapter provides an overview of visual language in order to give the beginning video journalist the fundamentals of cinematography, including the elements of shot sizes, composition, camera movement, and lighting. I'll focus the first half of the chapter on shot composition and camera movement, and then go into lighting in the second part.

Just as there are some prose writers who don't grab our attention, there are others who know how to use words to craft compelling stories. A good video journalist must learn to use the vocabulary of cinema in order to shape meaningful stories in a compelling way. The following basic cinema vocabulary and the accompanying exercises are designed to help you become a stronger video journalist.

> **Tip: It's Not the Shots, but the Story, Says Dai Sugano**
>
> Dai Sugano of the *San Jose Mercury News* discusses how video is a "new tool" for telling stories, but viewers are not impressed with the type of camera used to shoot the project. Rather, Sugano contends, "They care about stories. They care about the results, what kind of story you can tell."[4] No matter how good or bad your shot, interview, or audio, if the story isn't there, the audience isn't going to care. Indeed, an audience will tend to forgive poorer-quality production values—the quality of the shots and sounds—when you have a compelling story, than if you get everything perfect, but the story is weak.

The Importance of Cinematography

Cinematography isn't a style just for filmmakers. The word literally means to "write in motion" and, with the word's relationship to photography, it also means to "write in light." Some of the best video journalism pieces—whether work by Dai Sagano of the *San Jose Mercury News* or Travis Fox formerly of the *Washington Post*—are shot by trained photographers, those who have a keen understanding of composition, the properties of light, and the body language of their subjects—the visual emotional element of a human being doing something, wanting something, or needing something. They understand the pain, joy, duplicity—the entire ramification of the human condition—and their images place us into another person's intimate space formerly seen only by close friends and relatives. It is the private made public and the video journalist, in order to record compelling video, needs to build trust with her subject, a trust that gives permission for an audience to enter another person's personal space. The lens is an extension of the video journalist—so trust is imperative. The lens records what the video journalist feels, sees, and hears moment by moment. This comprises the craft of cinematography. The term videographer I relegate to camera operators who do not *feel* or build trust with their subjects and tend to express a form of recording that collects images and audio in order to fulfill the needs of what's in a script (shooting to script, collecting b-roll, shooting wall paper—images and sounds that are neither character centered, nor story centered, but rather illustrate a script with no strong sense of artistry). Cinematographers[5] tend to use lenses to "paint with light and shadow" as a means to elucidate the emotional core of characters in a story. They use the camera lens to open up and reveal the human condition in a visually compelling way. They're artists who reveal emotional truth through the lens of a camera with a keen awareness of how light and color and shadow shape the mood of a scene no less than how a painter approaches a canvas.

In the language of cinematography, video journalists must understand how different types of lenses create depth of field for focusing (fast lenses, with the iris wide open will provide a nice depth of field). They must learn how shot sizes render the sense of emotion—from close-ups to wide full shots, and how these shots render deep and flat space, as well as key visual components of who and what are in a scene. They must understand principles of composition—while at the same time understanding how light, shadow, and color reveal the emotional hues of characters in a story. With a variety of shots to choose from, shots that are designed to help move the story forward, the video journalist has a much easier time when editing, for the visual elements will be there to help structure the story.

HOW TO THINK ABOUT COMPOSITION AND CAMERA MOVEMENT

In order to become a good video journalist, you must begin to master the basic tools of cinematography:

- shot sizes and camera angles (composition)
- camera movement.

Before even worrying about lighting, it's important to master the visual storytelling tools of composition and how to move the composition through camera movement. Also, I'll examine in the case study how Travis Fox uses lines and space to his advantage in shaping his compositions.

Rule of Thirds

One of the fundamental rules of composition stems from the rule of thirds—a tool that closely aligns to the golden mean, a geometric pattern found in nature that can be mathematically derived. In short, by placing subjects along patterns of thirds (both vertically and horizontally), we can begin to discover how Fox shaped his composition through the rule of thirds.

Figure 3.1 Rule of thirds helps shape composition. Here, we can see how the subject's eyes are along the top third horizontal line. At the same time, the vertical line provides a rule of third with the main subject positioned screen left along that vertical. Most cameras include a rule of thirds pattern, so you can use it until it starts becoming instinctual.

Shot Sizes and Camera Angles

Shot sizes are the basic vocabulary of the filmmaker. They indicate actual or relative perception of distance of the subject to the audience. Wide-angle shots will tend to make the background seem more distant, while a telephoto shot (long lens or zoomed all the way in) will tend to compress the space, making the background appear closer than it is. Practice shooting with different lenses (or from wide to telephoto) so you can begin to see how the composition changes. Below, I'll use examples from Travis Fox's *narcocorrido* ballad story, which I'll present in full following shot sizes, camera angles, and camera movement. I want to lay out the shot size definitions, first, before going into it. I'll then discuss lighting and use Fox's "Crisis in Darfur Expands: Testimonials" as a case study in using natural light.

Wide or Long

Includes the space and full height of the subject. Some use this as a way to establish the space, but there are many video stories that start with close-ups, as in Fox's story on women in China.

Tends to provide emotional distance from the subject, and can be used for good emotional effect when the audience needs to "breathe" or reflect after an intense story moment.

Medium

The standard conversational shot. We're closer to the subject, entering a comfortable emotional zone—equivalent to standing or sitting next to someone and engaging in a conversation.

Use when you want to provide a sense of normalcy in a shot, in between strong emotional moments. Also, utilize when shooting "two shots"—two subjects in the shot at the same time.

Close-up

Used to create intimacy. In real life we only encounter the equivalent of this shot when standing close to someone—putting us toe-to-toe.

This shot conveys intimacy with the subject and presents a sense of shared trust—as if we're "in" on the "secret" of the conversation.

Even-level Angle

These three shots are all even level, providing a sense of emotional stability in the scene. It is what appears normal in our everyday experiences.

Big or Tight Close-up

We're more than close; we're in someone's face. This closeness usually occurs in moments of strong emotional intimacy or during a fight. Here, we get the sense that this singer is singing to us, personally.

Low Angle

The low-angle shot tends to give the subject power—at least from the audience's perspective, since it conveys a sense of the audience "looking up" to the subject.
It can also provide energy to the shot—especially when followed by an even-level shot, because it breaks how we perceive a subject normally, providing a new way of seeing. It is not often we lay on the floor and look up at a drummer, for example. By utilizing this shot, Fox energizes the scene and conveys an emotional truth—a new way of looking at the subject.

Extreme Close-up

Scenes can gain energy when they're broken down into pieces and then edited together. By shooting extreme close-ups, such as fingers strumming a bass, as we see here, it provides visual detail that we would never see live, unless we're the one performing.

Useful in cut-away shots in editing to mold moments of tension and release in a scene.

Camera Movement

There are several ways to move a camera—whether you're using a tripod or not. You can pan a camera left to right or right to left—rotating it on a horizontal axis. If you're shooting handheld, rotate your hips and that'll give you your pan. It is usually used to shift the story focus from one shot to another without cutting. You can also tilt a camera up or down, bending it along a vertical axis. If you're shooting handheld, then tilting would occur when you bow down or bend your body. However, these types of shots maintain relative motion in the foreground and background, so it can look unnatural, even unprofessional (same with using the zoom function on a camera). However, if you move the camera forward or backward, or track to the side (even if done by walking), then the foreground will appear to be moving faster than the background, and it will appear natural, more professional (especially if your moves are smooth!). Same thing when you move your arms up or down for a crane/jib type shot. If you practice with these, your work can improve. Go to the equipment page of the book's website (www.kurtlancaster.com/equipment/), and you can look at what's called a pocket dolly traveler, which attaches to a tripod and allows you to create tracking and dolly type shots in the field without a lot of extra gear.

Pan (Left and Right)

A pan will allow an audience to follow eye lines of what a subject is looking at as well as provide movement energy to a shot, picking up one action by following another. It allows for a reframing of shot sizes as well, as in the case of Fox, who captures an action in a medium shot to a close-up by panning his camera left to pick up the couple dancing in the foreground.

Michael Rabiger in *Directing the Documentary* (Focal Press, 2009) says that the

real-life equivalency of the pan includes: "Taking in one's surroundings; comprehending; discovering; revealing; escaping; assessing; fearing, expecting" (p. 103).

Tilt up and Tilt down

In this shot, Fox actually panned right while tilting the camera up in order to maintain a smoothness of energy of the beating drum and the visual rhythm of the dancers in the foreground.

The tilt-up typically energizes a scene by shifting our focus down or level to a position up, as if we, as the audience, are tilting our heads.

It's a way to not only shift our focus from one shot to another without using a cut during editing, but also shifting the energy of the scene, and therefore our perception of what is occurring in the story.

A tilt-up will tend to empower (engage), while a tilt-down will tend to weaken (turn away), depending on the context of the story.

Rabiger describes these kinds of shots as "Assessing height or depth; looking up to; looking down on; threatening or feeling threatened" (p. 103). See his book for a table of how "cinema language parallels human experience," as he puts it (Rabiger 2009: 103–104).

Push in and Pull out

If you walk towards your subject, you are pushing into that subject's space, and the shot size will change from a wide shot to a close-up, depending on where you started in the frame and where you decide to stop. Moving forward will energize a scene, slowly lending emotional energy to a scene as you start wide and go close.

If you start close, and pull out, often the energy deflates, which is useful when you are modulating the tension and release in a scene. The pull-out will tend to release. However, if the pull-out reveals something new, it may actually lend energy to the scene.

CASE STUDY 1—SHAPING A VISUAL STORY THROUGH SHOT COMPOSITION AND CAMERA MOVEMENT IN TRAVIS FOX'S "*NARCOCORRIDOS* AND NIGHTLIFE IN MEXICALI"

Here, I'll examime how a master video journalist thinks about shooting video, and, through an examination of his video, show how Fox managed to create a strong piece of documentary journalism by looking at how he structured his story through visual storytelling—controlling not only his composition, shot sizes, and camera movement, but also how he utilized the space in helping to shape the form of visual storytelling. I witnessed Fox shoot this video in Mexicali in the summer of 2009.

In a Mexicali bar after 10 p.m. on a Friday night. Fox talks to a variety of characters before pulling out a camera. It's basic reporting skills at work. He needs to get a sense of the story, first, before shooting. He needs to know what characters he'll use in his piece. After getting the lay of the land, Fox pulls out his camera, checks its settings, and tends to bring the camera in close, his shotgun microphone attached to the top of the camera. In a loud environment, such as this bar, he has no choice—if the shotgun mic isn't close enough to his subjects, he won't get clear enough sound from his interviewees. At the same time, he chooses a variety of shot sizes and angles. To get the angle he wants for his story, he'll even sit on the floor, angling his camera up at his subjects. All his shots are handheld and he uses available natural light in the space (he changes the color to black and white in post in order to compensate for the poor lighting in the space). Although trained as a photographer, Fox received no formal training in video. He learned on the job at the *Washington Post* by playing with one of their video cameras in 1999.

> This was before people were watching web video, before my editors were watching web video, even. So that went on for a couple years. I was able to learn on my own terms without having anyone see it. You know, thank God, because it was bad. But I was able to do it, and the fact that I was editing—I was learning kind of what I needed. So I would go out and shoot, go out and report, and then when I would come back to edit, I wouldn't necessarily have all the pieces to make a story, and then I realized [I need to shoot more], and that's how I learned—from editing and constructing a story.

When a video journalist goes out into the field, Fox feels they should have a sense of the visual story in their head, the images needed to edit a story together. They may have the essence of the story, itself, but Fox learned that, when editing in his early days, he discovered he was missing shots, like a "transition, I can't move from here to here" when he edited it. He also learnt the importance of asking the right "types of questions and the types of information that works best" for video. Furthermore, unlike reporting through writing, it's very difficult to go back and shoot what you're missing. As Fox puts it,

> With video you really have to know what your story is while you're doing it, and you can't just go and talk to a lot of other people. Your story can't really change after the fact. It can to a certain extent [through editing], and you shouldn't lock yourself in [to one kind of edit], but you have to get all the pieces you need.

It's difficult to go back to a shoot. "If you don't have all the pieces," he adds, describing the limitation of reporting for video journalism, "you can't make a couple of phone calls later the next day, and change it around. It doesn't work that way, so in that sense it's a different way of reporting. In that way, it's limiting."

Thus, a good video journalist should know the sense of the shots needed to tell the story in order to have the right material to edit—asking the right questions to help construct the story. And a video journalist should do their own editing in order to control the story. Fox explains, "We have journalists that are doing video, then they hand over the tape, and someone else edits it." Fox believes that this is a mistake, "because then they don't really learn hands-on what they need, and they don't understand how the pieces cut together. So if you don't have all the right shots, then the cuts don't work."

Shot List and Transcript

Below, I include a frame from the first second of each shot of Fox's video, including a description of the shot size and camera angle for each, as well as a transcript of the song and dialogue from the subjects he interviewed.

Shot variety

Examining "*Narcocorridos* and Nightlife in Mexicali," we can see the variety of shots Fox collected. From the eighteen different shots, he edited together twenty-one cuts (twenty-three when including the two pans to reframe a shot). We can see the pattern he utilized in his finished edit:

> wide or long—1, 18
> medium wide—3, 10, 16, 19B, 21
> medium—2, 5, 7, 11, 14, 20A
> close-up—4, 8, 9, 12, 13, 17, 20B
> big and extreme close-ups—6, 15, 19A.

Furthermore, not only does he shoot a variety of shot sizes, but he also shoots them from a variety of angles:

> even (lens level with horizon line)—1, 3, 4, 6, 8–10, 18, 19B, 20A
> low—2, 7, 11, 12, 15, 16, 20B, 21
> extremely low—5, 14, 17
> high—13, 19A.

He also tilts the camera angle off the vertical axis in: 7, 15, 17, 19A, 20A, 20B, 21.
From the final edit, we can see that Fox used only a few shots more than once:

> 1 and 18
> 2, 7, and 20A
> 4 and 9.

| 1. Wide |
| Even level angle |

Narcocorridos song (translated from Spanish) sung by the group, Los Villanos del Norte:

"When he was young, he sold oranges in the mountains . . ."

| 2. Medium |
| Slight low angle |

". . . in order just to eat. He's never embarrassed because of that. He's proud of it."

| 3. Medium wide |
| Even level angle |

Singer: I just sing what I hear on TV and the radio, but we just make it rhyme.

| 4. Close up |
| Even level angle |

| 5. Medium |
| Extreme low angle |

Song: "He's part of the most powerful cartel . . ."

6. Extreme close-up
   Even level angle

". . . and of course he's from Culiacan.
He flies its flag. He's always proud.
He says, I'm Chapo Guzman!"

...and of course he's from Culiacan.

7. Medium
   Low angle

He flies its flag. He's always proud.

8. Close up
   Even level angle

It's the most popular music...

Singer: It's the most powerful music.
It's what people want to listen to.

9. Close up
   Even level angle

...it's what people want to listen to.

10. Medium wide
    Even level angle

The people who come to night clubs want this music.

Singer: The people who come to night clubs
want this music. They ask for *narco-corridos*.

| 11. Medium |
| Low angle |

Customer: Some of the drug lords are like our, like our Robin Hood in Mexico. Even though they do crazy things—illegal stuff—they help the people.

| 12. Close |
| Low angle |

| 13. Close up |
| High angle |

Song: "It's known that he's quiet and short but he's got a smart head. He's a humanitarian. He's benevolent."

| 14. Medium |
| Extreme low angle |

Singer interview (VO): Even in Los Angeles, what people see on the street becomes music.

| 15. Big close up |
| Low angle |

16. Medium wide
    Low angle

Singer interview (VO): Here in Mexico, it's the same.

17. Close up
    Extreme low angle

Singer interview (VO): What we see becomes "corridos." In that way, *corridos* are similar to rap music.

18. Wide
    Even level angle

19a. Big close up
     High angle
     Pan and tilt up to

Sound of music and dancing through to end.

19b. Medium wide
     Even level angle

20a. Medium
      Even level angle
      Pan left to foreground

20b. Close up
      Low angle

21. Medium wide
     Low angle

This means that Fox used nineteen original shots with four different angles, and five different shot sizes, for the 2:28 short documentary. Shot variety in visual storytelling is a fundamental tool of the documentary journalist.

Principle of Contrast and Affinity

What do the variety of shot sizes and camera angles mean? Why would a video journalist need to gather so many different kinds of shots in order to help make a good piece? Bruce Block, in his important book, *The Visual Story: Creating the Visual Structure of Film, TV, and Digital Media* (Focal Press, 2008), discusses the key to good visual storytelling. It's tied to "the intensity, or dynamic, of the audience's emotional reaction" (p. 11), which is related to the "Principle of Contrast & Affinity":

> The greater the contrast in a visual component, the more the visual intensity or dynamic increases. The greater the affinity in a visual component, the more the visual intensity or dynamic decreases (Block 2008: 11).

In visual media, such as film and video, Block believes that the creator can apply this principle to space, line and shape, tone, color, movement, and visual rhythm in order to help induce an emotional reaction in the audience: "The audience's reaction can be emotional (they cry, laugh, or scream) or physical (their muscles tense up, they cover their eyes, they fall asleep). Usually the more intense the visual stimulus, the more intense the audience reaction" (Block 2008: 11).

We can see how Fox—whether consciously or unconsciously—utilizes Block's principle of visual contrast and affinity. In the first three shots, we see Fox go from a wide, medium, to a medium wide; with shots 1 and 3 he shoots at an even level, while the second shot is a low angle.

The principle of contrast and affinity applies to the content of a shot, as well as the energy it creates from shot to shot. Also, take note of Fox's composition—he makes shot 3 a medium shot, not shooting wide, which may have captured the ceiling. This composition reinforces the flatness of the space, but the horizontal line halfway down the frame divides dark and light tones, providing contrast within the shot. Notice how the left foreground individual's dark shirt blends into the darker tone of the wall in the background. In documentary journalism, there is little the journalist can do to change this. If this were a fictional film shoot, the costume designer would make sure that the tonal quality of the clothing wouldn't blend with the tonal quality of the wall—unless the story needed it. Also note how the darker hair of the individuals on the left provides contrast to the light part of the wall creating more visual intensity than the woman on the right, whose blonde hair highlighting her right side blends into the tonal quality of the wall. These are the kinds of details that a video journalist should begin to notice and utilize as a way of helping to shape the flow of visual intensity.

Shot 1 Travis Fox shoots at an even-level angle. Looking at the use of space and tone, visually we see the first shot engaging deep space—the lights in the background providing bright contrast to the darker foreground—which helps provide depth to the composition, the lines receding along the edge of the ceiling and walls, again reinforcing depth according to Bruce Block (2008: 14–27; 120–130).

When he was young, he sold oranges in the mountains...

Shot 2 Fox then cuts to the medium shot of the singer, whose engaging performance captures the attention of the viewer. Note how he's framed by the walls in a darker tone with the doorway, brightly lit. The singer has a darker tone, so he stands in contrast to the bright background—all of which provides visual intensity to the shot. Notice also how Fox utilizes the existing light source from the right side, the location of the bar, and how it hits the singer's arm. In addition, the light on the wall separates the performer from the background. If there were no existing backlight, the shot would be far less dynamic.

He's pround of it.

Shot 3 In the third shot, the patrons are against a wall that has no receding lines—it is a flat space, which is in contrast to the previous two shots engaging deep space. Because of this fact, the sequence of shots lends themselves to more dynamic intensity, than if this shot repeated the sense of depth (three shots leading to an affinity of space, despite the fact that deep space is more dynamic than flat space).

The Visual Hook

These three shots comprise the hook of the piece. The music draws us in and the third shot shows customers laughing, having a good time, the emotional reaction—as edited—to the musicians' song. (Indeed, the third shot may have come later in the evening, since it was shot at a different time than when Fox shot the musicians' song.) In either case, the reaction shot—the reaction to the action—is key in good visual storytelling, since the reaction is what the storyteller uses to create the feeling he or she wants the audience to experience.

If Fox had used three shots of the same size and angle, then, according to Block, we would have less dynamic intensity, affinity breeding lethargy in the piece and probably in the audience. But, by choosing shots that are unlike each other, the contrast engages visual intensity and helps induce emotional intensity in the audience. Because Fox knows he'll be later editing this piece, he collects a variety of shots, taken from different angles and sizes just so that he will have more choices when structuring the emotional core of the story during editing. If he had only shot from a half dozen different angles—and in the hands of a less-skilled cinematographer that might have been the case—then the overall video would lack the dynamism it expresses. One may have shot the band in a wide shot, and maybe shot a couple of medium shots of the musicians playing, such as shot 2, then the story would be much weaker, due to Block's principle of contrast and affinity—not enough shot variety to shape the ebb and flow of visual intensity, which is tied to the emotional shape of the story.

As Fox notes:

> You want to start strong visually, and with a strong hook that you're going to hook your audience with early on. You know, there's a rule: start with your best stuff. It's literally that simple. It's a similar kind of narrative structure where you have the rising and the climax and all of that. I don't think all news pieces have those elements, of course, but ideally you have those elements, and then you have a nice kind of kicker at the end, a nice little bow that you tie it up with, a little present at the end, and then you're out.

Building Visual Intensity

By shooting musicians playing from a variety of angles and shot sizes, Fox helps create visual intensity in his piece. The close-ups and low angles in both of these sequences lend energy to the scene, shaping the emotions of the audience dynamically, which would not have occurred if Fox had shot similar shot sizes and angles. In shot 15, we see tonal affinity between the performer and the back wall. The single strand of light Fox captures—the diagonal cutting upscreen rights—helps guide the viewer's eye to the singer, who has a little wash of fill light come from screen left onto his cheek.

Utilizing Lines and Angles for Visual Storytelling

Also take note as to the strong lines and angles Fox engages. Dynamically, Block explains how horizontel lines contain the least amount of visual energy, the vertical contains more, while the diagonal burns strongest (2008: 88–114). Thus, in shot 15, the diagonal light lends energy to the scene. Other diagonals include the angle of the bass being played by the musician in shots 14 and 17. Also, in 16, we can see how Fox composed the low angle of the drummer to include diagonals of the ceiling converging in a brightly lit corner.

He intercuts these two diagonally framed musical sequences with the singer's interview (shot 9), audience reactions (shot 10), a cutaway to the toy monkey (shot 11), and an interview with an audience member (shot 12). These shots are a bit less dynamic than the sequence that precedes it (shots 5–8). Yet, notice how Fox uses corners and lines to help shape the dynamic energy in each shot. Shot 9 is framed from the left side, capturing the diagonal of the wall as it recedes to the corner behind the musician, and his bass is used as a line to help frame him along the rule of thirds. Similarly, in the next shot, two audiences singing along at a table are framed screen right, with lines receding to the corner in the background. They're framed oppositely from shot 9, creating visual contrast in framing. If the subjects in shot 10 were framed screen left, the shot would have been in visual affinity with shot 9, and would have lessened the visual intensity. In the next two shots (11 and 12), we see both the monkey and the customer being framed center. The monkey is framed in the corner, the diagonal of the beer can and the torso parallel to the corner, as light shines down from above, providing stark contrast of tone. In shot 12, we can see how Fox not only framed the man in the center of the screen, helping to create visual similarity in the previous shot as a way to transition us from the musicians and the other audience members, but he also utilizes the lines of the light to dynamically compose him against the ceiling and walls, placing it in a deep spatial shot. It's one of the most powerful shots of the piece and it comes at the same moment that he talks about how some drug lords are "like our Robin Hood in Mexico. Even though they do crazy things—illegal stuff—they help the people." It's a controversial statement, coming about half-way through the piece, but that statement—arresting as it is—is even stronger, because it's tied to the dynamic energy of how he is visually framed by Fox.

Story Intensity = Visual Intensity

The story intensity should be tied to the visual intensity, simultaneously, otherwise the story becomes deflated.

The final sequence follows the even stronger dynamic intensity of the singers intercut with their audience dancing (18–21). The wide shot of the bar, shot 18, provides a transition.

Camera Movement

Fox takes the only two panning shots in the piece and saves them for the end (shots 19, 20), creating one of the strongest visually compelling moments due to the fact the camera moves. Note, also, how the two pans are in opposite directions, helping to create visual intensity from the contrast of camera movement. It shapes a strong resolution, as he creates this dance sequence for nearly thirty seconds with no dialogue.

Also take note how Fox did not write any narration, instead relying on his interview subjects to tell the story in their own words—he knew the kinds of questions to ask that would help shape the story structure from the people he interviewed. The song-centered piece lends itself for a short documentary not needing any narration.

Tip: "10 Golden Rules for Video Journalists" by Travis Fox

Travis Fox's ten golden rules of shooting video (Wu 2009):

- **Golden Rule 10**: Get "X-roll." X-roll is when you get your interviewee's money quotes in their natural environment
- **Golden Rule 9**: Shoot within 180 degrees around a subject. In other words, don't walk around your subject when interviewing them
- **Golden Rule 8**: Sequence your video with a variety of detail, tight, medium, wide shots as well as cut away shots. 50 percent of shots will be tight, 25 percent medium and 25 percent wide
- **Golden Rule 7**: Remember 80:20 ratio (80 percent should be b-roll and 20 percent should be interviews)
- **Golden Rule 6**: Get close to the subject when interviewing them for audio purposes
- **Golden Rule 5**: Stay quiet when shooting
- **Golden Rule 4**: If you do not get the shot, you do not have it
- **Golden Rule 3**: Do not move the camera when shooting (unless you are an advanced videographer)
- **Golden Rule 2**: Hold every shot for 10 seconds
- **Golden Rule 1**: Wear headphones

INTRODUCTION TO LIGHTING

Look and Feel

There's not space in this book to present a full overview of lighting, but I'll touch upon a few ideas to get you started about thinking how to use available light on your shoots in order to improve the look of your video. There is a list of books at the end of the chapter for further reading.

Light and shadow shape how an audience perceives images, whether in art, photography, or film. In video, lighting can sometimes be tough—it's not as forgiving as film. In film schools, cinematographers are taught how to use lights to shape the look and feel of the scenes they shoot. It's rare that video journalists carry around light kits, but a basic understanding of how to shape existing light is crucial when trying to make your work stand out and express a professional look.

The "look" of a video comprises how we perceive the image against the eyes. It's what we see in a shot.

The "feel" of the video stems from what we emotionally perceive in the shot.

Light and shadow shape how we see images and what we feel about those images. It's a balance between crafting a functional image that can be seen and the aesthetic beauty that makes the image stand out as something special.

How to Shoot Outdoors

Travis Fox, in his piece, "Crisis in Darfur Expands: Testimonials," masterfully used sunlight to his advantage. When shooting outdoors, you're working with sunlight—the sun may be diffused by clouds, providing a softer look for the images (where the shadows are not as sharp). It's best to shoot earlier in the morning or later in the afternoon, so you have more shadow to work with and the light quality is warmer. In Figure 3.2, we can see how Fox chose to keep his subjects' backs to the sun and shoot a wide shot of children singing in the camp, with some others playing basketball in the background. The sunlight captures the colors of the children in the foreground, and the browns of the sand provide a warm tone in contrast to the blue sky above. The sun is harsh, providing strong shadows, but he exposed his camera properly, closing up the iris in order to block out as much sun so the subjects stand out and the sky is not overexposed (blown out).

Figure 3.2 Travis Fox presents a wide shot of children singing and some playing basketball in the background. The shot has good exposure from the sky to the sands. The dark skin of the characters is underexposed as a result, since video can't cover the full exposure range in sunlight.

How to Use Key, Fill, and Backlighting: the Three-Point Lighting Model

With the indoor shot (Figure 3.3), Fox has chosen an angle and positioned his subject so that light from screen left becomes the *key* or main light source—the light is motivated and it comes from the sunlight streaming in from the left of the tent. This light also hits the wall in the background, the light reflecting off from it, becoming *background* light. Some of this reflected light falls onto the side of the character's face, screen right, catching some light in his eye. This is the *fill* light. Notice that the shadows are not strong—they're diffused. This provides a softer quality to the shot.

Figure 3.3 Travis Fox presents a close-up with three-point lighting.

When shooting subjects indoors, move the subject and/or existing lamps in order to place a "key" or main source of the light, such as a window or lamp, and light one side of a subject's face. Use reflected light to help fill in the other side of the face—it should be dimmer and the fill light helps fill in the shadows caused by the key light. If needed, use another existing lamp. It may be worth purchasing an LED light powered by batteries in order to use that as a key or fill light. For ethical considerations, would moving a subject to get better light break journalistic integrity? If the emotional truth of the story—the content—isn't altered, I would argue "no." However, if adding a light alters how the subject behaves, then perhaps ethical lines are being crossed.

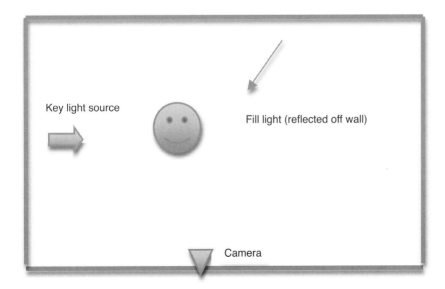

Figure 3.4 Top-view floor plan of Fox's close-up of the boy. The camera is center, facing the subject. There is a key light coming screen left, hitting the subject and the back wall. Fill light bounces from the back wall onto the screen right side of the subject.

CASE STUDY 2: LIGHTING IN TRAVIS FOX'S "CRISIS IN DARFUR EXPANDS: TESTIMONIALS"

http://vimeo.com/1293941

Let's see how Travis Fox puts these visual elements altogether in his work, "Crisis in Darfur Expands: Testimonials" (6:04), the *Washington Post* (March 7, 2007). As a video journalist, Fox was given the time to go deeper into his story, an approach he could never do in a breaking news story, for example. Rather, it's an "evergreen" topic where, Fox says, they were given the "resources and time to do that project. I was there for two weeks working on it, and I was editing for another two weeks when I got back, so it's a lot of time and effort." This allowed his visual work to be "linked to many articles over time," taking advantage of the web presence, which also helped "get page views over time, which it did," Fox adds (interview with the author, July 2009).

Fox would earn a Concentra Award nomination for outstanding video journalism for his work on "Crisis in Darfur Expands." He sets up the hook with a spanning shot of the refugee camp, followed by children singing. The introduction shows images of a refugee camp—a windswept desert, children singing, playing ball, an expanse of refugee tents in Chad—all of which revolve around a variety of shot sizes, angles, and dissolves. No narration. The desert landscapes and the shots of Amina Abakr's tent comprising the first ten shots last forty seconds. The images set up a question as to what is going on and why we're being shown these compelling images. Fox doesn't speak a word, letting his lens do the talking for him.

Fox sets us up for the crisis point. We're not told that one of Anima Akabr's children dies in a Janjaweed attack until ninety seconds in, and we discover nearly twenty seconds later that her husband died. Fox is providing us with a witness testimonial, allowing his subject to speak in her own words, as he manipulates the images elicited by a cinematographer's eye and a rhythmic sense of pacing to strongly structure her testimonial around visually compelling images that show her living space, her emotion, and her children's intensity. See the pictures below (shots 17–19).

Fox's piece engages the voice of the mother, who talks about wanting to protect her children. She stops talking, and Fox holds the tight close-up for four seconds. It's followed by shots 18 and 19, where no dialogue is spoken. Just the natural sound of wind flapping the tent, providing the audience with a moment of emotional release (an editing technique covered in Chapter 5).

No words are spoken for eight seconds. But we see a tight close-up of the mother, followed by a low angle three-shot of her children, followed by a tight close-up of one of her sons. Note how a single side key light, screen left in shots 18 and 19, is provided by the sun cutting through the back area of the tent, with fill light provided as bounced light from the bricks of the wall (which also acts as a back light). Abakr has a key three-quarters front, with backlight from the wall.

Fox didn't just use a camera to make this piece of video journalism. He knew the right points to light. He understands three-point lighting and he knows how to utilize it when getting his shots, one by one.

Another powerful moment (shot 6) includes a crossfade of a wide shot of children singing to a low-angle long-lens shot of the desert ground with debris blowing in the wind, buildings

17   18

19

Shots 17, 18, 19 Travis Fox utilizes lighting, shot sizes, and silence to create a powerful moment.

out of focus in the background, followed by a blur of footsteps walking by close to the lens—the song slowly fades as harsh wind noises increase in volume.

Not only does Fox have a sense of timing to his cuts, but he also knows how to use natural sound to shape the emotional experience of the viewer—a key element in strong filmmaking, in which both visual and audio are used in conjunction to shape the story. The documentary journalism style practiced by Fox in this piece reveals somebody who uses most of the tools of filmmaking in order to shape his story, creating an emotional experience for the audience—tools of cinematography, editing, dialogue, and sound design. In Fox's work I don't feel he privileges one tool of filmmaking over another. Rather, he uses the tools available to him and makes his editing decisions based on the content of the story. Stark desert shots and the orange glow of lighting in the tent provide us with two contrasting visuals shaping the two themes of the work: despair and hope. I'm allowed to draw that conclusion, due to the fact that Fox didn't tell me to think this way.

Let's map Fox's story structure for this first testimonial on the story graph (see Figure 3.5).

The hook is the beautiful desert landscape and the children singing. The beauty draws us in. The introduction or exposition includes shots of the location, the goats passing, the blowing desert sand, and the exterior of Abakr's tent. It sets the stage without any kind of spoon-feeding by Fox. The conflict begins when we see the tiny housing for Abakr and her children. We hear her story, about how she lost a child. We see shots of the children spaced in a way to help build tension. The climax occurs as a tight close-up on Abakr's face, who says she never got to see her husband after he was killed by the Janjaweed. Fox cuts to the medium wide of the camp, as we hear her say that some people buried her husband's body on the spot. The section lasts two minutes.

Shot 6 Travis Fox utilizes sound design, such as this moment with blowing dust and debris to create a cinematic moment.

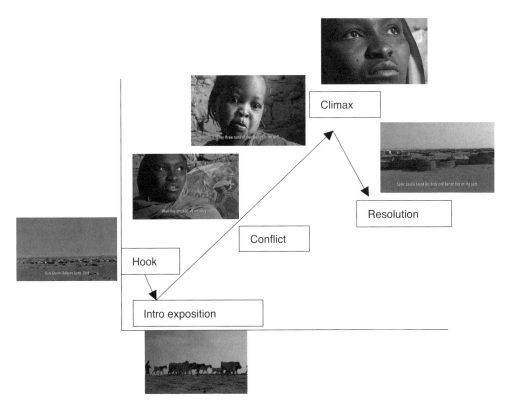

Figure 3.5 The story structure graph from Travis Fox's "Crisis in Darfur Expands: Testimonials."

SHOOTING EXERCISE 1: COMPOSITION AND CINEMATOGRAPHY IN USING SHOT SIZES

To learn how to use shot sizes, go to a friend's personal living space or workspace and shoot them doing an action. Shoot a series of 8–10 shots of one subject, but use different shot sizes and camera angles (keep the camera movement/motion minimal or still, such as with a tripod or steady handheld, but the subject may move). Be sure to capture the subject doing something (actions), as well as capturing shots of their living space or workspace. Be sure to shoot the action from a variety of angles and shot sizes. Get in close! Cover only one location, one subject, and one consecutive moment in time. No dialogue. No audio. Turn automatic camera settings off—learn to control your camera manually, so you can have full control over the look of your shots. Also, use close-ups at moments of heightened emotional moments or tension. Don't forget to control what's in the shot, framing only what you want your audience to see. Intercut the action shots with the interview using only 10 to 20 percent of the character on screen, but use the voice beneath the cutaway shots.

After you've recorded it, put it together and edit it. Watch how the different shots capture the action of your subject and how it conveys emotion. Try shooting a variety of angles and shot sizes of the same action and, when editing, move the shots around. Play with it. Get a sense of how the story changes when the shot sizes and angles change. If you begin to feel bored, then you're staying on the shot too long or you've created a series of shots that are of the same size and/or angle. Change it up—but only during shifting emotional moments. If you change it up for no story reason, then it'll appear random and unmotivated. Motivate the shots by linking them to progressing story moments.

SHOOTING EXERCISE 2: CAMERA MOVEMENT

Drawing on your personal themes, shoot two people engaged in a conversation. Use a variety of shot sizes and camera angles to tell the story visually. At one or two places—when the conversation is the most animated or emotional—move the camera, such as pushing in or pulling out. Reveal an emotional shift in a character with camera movement.

SHOOTING EXERCISE 3: LIGHTING 1

Shoot a subject sitting inside an office or at home. First, just shoot ten seconds without paying attention to any lighting. Open or close the iris in order to properly expose the subject you're shooting. Next, add a key light—place the subject near a window from either the left or right side. Shoot ten seconds. Next, add to this a background light—it can be a light hitting a back wall or a light turned in the background. This will provide depth to the shots. Shoot ten seconds. Lastly, add a fill light—either using light bounced off a back wall, use a reflector, or use an existing lamp or an LED light to bounce light onto the subject on the opposite side of the key light source. Don't place an LED lamp on the camera, but use it to bounce off of a wall, using it as a fill. Shoot another ten seconds. Take a look at what you've shot. Use the camera's LCD screen to help you get the look and feel of the scene you want. Think about how the feeling of the story changes when you add and take away lights. Experiment. If your light is hitting a subject directly, then it's going to evoke a hard light source with a lot of strong shadows. If you're bouncing light onto a subject, the shadows will be softer—it provides a soft-light quality. You're not just making light functional, but you're trying to evoke an emotion that reflects the emotional core of the story. Fox's image in the refugee camp in Darfur—with the strong shadows—tends to evoke a somber mood.

SHOOTING EXERCISE 3: LIGHTING 2

Shoot with natural light indoors. Use Fox's shot of the boy as your inspiration. Find a diffused key light (such as a sheet blocking the direct sunlight) and position the subject so it becomes a key side light. Use a reflector or bounced light from a wall as a fill and be sure it's opposite to the key and that the fill is darker than the key. (If it's the same intensity, then the image will maintain a flat, non-cinematic look.) Also, frame your subject so there is depth in the shot (not a flat wall). If you can shoot it with a shallow depth of field, even better. To get a shallow depth of field outside, open your iris all the way and either add neutral density filters (or switch it on) or increase your shutter speed.

CINEMATOGRAPHY WORKSHEET

I break this worksheet into two sections: Composition and Lighting. Each will provide material you will want to consider when shooting a project—both from a technical and an artistic standpoint.

Composition

- ✧ What character actions, objects, settings, and interviews can you potentially shoot? Make a list.
- ✧ What shot composition (shot size, camera angle, and content) will best convey the interviews and actions of the character(s)? Make a shot list describing the shot size and what actions will be captured in your composition.
- ✧ Identify the shot size and angle (low, normal, high).
- ✧ Describe the actions in the shot.
- ✧ Furthermore, identify whether the shot will be against a flat space or deep space.
- ✧ Also, should the shot be in deep focus or shallow focus?
- ✧ For deep focus, close up the aperture (you may need to add more light), and/or a wide to normal lens.
- ✧ For shallow focus, open up the aperture and/or a long (telephoto lens); if you're outdoors and you can't open the iris without overexposing the shot, increase the shutter speed to compensate.
- ✧ Make a note in your shot list of the possible decisive moments. Does the composition best serve the decisive moment?
- ✧ What kind of camera movement is needed to help visualize the story (this is when you change composition within the same shot)?
- ✧ What lenses do you need to best serve the composition of each shot? Wide, normal, telephoto?
- ✧ If you're using a zoom lens, don't zoom during a shot—use the zoom as a convenience for changing your composition! Frame the shot and then record. Moving shots are best served by wide and normal lenses.

Lighting

✦   What light quality do you need for the story? What will best convey the mood, energy, and style of the scene?

✦   Describe the emotional tones you're hoping to achieve in the scene.

✦   Draw a rough floor plan of each location you plan to shoot and identify existing light sources you can use, such as windows (tied to the time of day you're shooting) and practical lights.

✦   On the floor plan, identify:

- Key light
- Fill light
- Back/background lights.

✦   What do you need to add or take away in order to meet a three-point lighting setup? Identify additional equipment, such as reflectors or scrims you could use to bounce or diffuse light. In most cases, video journalists will not be adding lights or scrims or reflectors, if they're working solo, so you need to train your eye to use existing light sources like a master. Otherwise, bring the extra tools along, in case you need them. If you have a crew member, the reflector can be a useful tool to bounce light.

✦   Identify the color temperature of your key light and expose your camera for the key.

FOR FURTHER READING

Block, Bruce. *The Visual Story*. Focal Press, 2008. This is for advanced video journalists who want to understand how the concepts of art—line and shape, space, tone, color, and visual rhythm—can be used to shape the visual elements to the story elements in your doc. For those who want to become really good cinematographers. An understanding of Block's principle of contrast and affinity is essential in crafting powerful visual stories.

Lancaster, Kurt. *DSLR Cinema: Crafting the Film Look with Video*. Focal Press, 2011. For those of you shooting video with DSLRs, this book not only provides tips and tricks on using these cameras when shooting video, but provides the basics of lighting, as well, with examples of outdoor lighting.

Malkiewicz, Kris. *Film Lighting: Talks with Hollywood's Cinematographers and Gaffers*. New York Prentice Hall, 1986. This book includes interviews with master cinematographers in Hollywood. Their ideas on light and how it relates to story in a practical way will be useful for those who want to understand the nature of cinematography's art and craft.

Mercardo, Gustavo. *The Filmmaker's Eye: Learning (and Breaking) the Rules of Cinematic Composition*. Focal Press, 2011. A great text analyzing stills from films, covering all the basic shots and the reasons they work. Although all the examples are fiction, good documentary journalists can learn strong cinematic techniques from fiction and apply them to their nonfiction projects.

Interlude

Short Video Documentaries—From an Interview with Ann Derry, Video Director, the New York Times

As the director of video at the *New York Times*, Ann Derry must coordinate a large team of video shooters and think about a variety of styles to utilize in order to capture a variety of audiences. I spoke to Derry at the *Times* offices in New York City in July 2009.

INCREASED DEMAND FOR VIDEO

There's an increasing demand for and use for video journalism in newspaper websites. What I think is going to happen is people will become more video literate. It's happening in our newsroom—video's becoming a language, so I like to say language that reporters are now beginning to speak. There will be stories that lend themselves to video. And so those provide great storytelling opportunities. I think people are going to expect more and more to see video on newspaper websites. Print's not going to go away. And print journalism's not going to go away. [Video is] like another tool in the toolbox. And what I do think could end up happening, and it probably is already happening in places, is when you have unlimited resources you can do an article, a video, a multimedia presentation, a photo, a graphic. As resources become more constrained, and we become a more multimedia-friendly world, I think news organizations—whether they started out as radio or television or print—are going to look at the story and ask, "What's the best tool, what's the best medium for telling the story? Is it words? Is it pictures? Is it video? Is it a combination?" But it's not everything.

The *Times* was fairly smart and forward looking, because we integrated the web and the print side early. So that it gave not only video, but all the tools of the website became incorporated into the work flow of the print newsroom. And there's actually not a separate print newsroom and a web newsroom, but they're all the same. We all sit next to each other. The Video desk is in the newsroom next to the Photo desk, and next to the Culture desk. It's all integrated. I think that as the news business goes forward, as it evolves, and as the tools evolve, it becomes a part of that. I think [video is] an increasing part of it, but we didn't start out in it—we're not an image-based organization. Myself and my senior producers all come from television, so we worked in and for image-based organizations, video-based organizations. And it's different here. The infrastructure alone is enormous if you want to have a video-based organization. You need lines, you need camera people all over the place, you need satellite dishes. We don't have that to really cover the news. So I think that the *Times* is going to be a print and a text-based organization for a long time to come, especially in news coverage, and that the job—my job, especially—is to bring video, create this language in the newsroom, bring it forward, find ways to tell video stories, and then look for opportunities in places—in ways where we don't have a camera. For example, I don't have a camera on the Sotomayor [Supreme Court nomination] hearings in Washington, right? I don't have a camera in the room. There's a pool feed. We are tapped into that pool feed. In Iran, for example, I had a freelancer with a camera. But I didn't have a whole [news crew]—it wasn't like *NBC News* that had a satellite truck—so it's just different. We don't have [that kind of] infrastructure.

TURN A WEAKNESS INTO A STRENGTH

What you do is you take your weakness and you turn it into a strength. And so, part of it is we all come from—myself and my senior producers—documentary filmmaking television. So actually that's our first love. We started out doing *New York Times* television, and we made documentaries in the newsroom with the newsroom first, for five or six or seven years. So there's already a fair amount of television documentary expertise, both for ourselves and with the reporters. What we did is we took that interest, that expertise, and we said, "Okay. We're not going to make hour-long documentaries any more," which is just as well, because those are really hard to do with a breaking news organization. But we will do seven-minute pieces or five-minute pieces or ten-minute pieces. And they'll be more—and it's actually much easier than doing a full documentary. You can do it much more quickly; you can be working very organically—right inside the newsroom—with the reporters. And you do things like write, and you're sending one video journalist out with a reporter, they have small cameras—it's that whole kind of format that people have been using for a long time. And it's perfect for critical web video—it harkens all the way back to 16mm. And the way people started making documentaries and vérité filmmaking that's what they started with. They started with a camera and a soundman—very simple packages. And in a way what's happening is we're going back to that with just some better equipment.

We've been doing this for about three and a half years, so we've worked a lot on just trying to figure out what our styles are. And I would say that our enterprise documentary reporting style includes a video journalist going out with a reporter; you're there shooting in the field with them, you have a video journalist with a camera, and you then come back. You're putting together a piece—the reporter and the video journalists are working together. It's pretty much character driven and voices driven; it's what you've actually seen and found.

WORKING WITH REPORTERS

The reporter's rarely a character in the story, but the reporter tells the story. The reporter writes the narration with the video journalist. The reporter often voices the pieces, and I've increasingly asked people—reporters and video journalists—to actually have the reporter in the beginning introduce themselves, but it's all voice-over. You don't even see [the reporter]—so it's a little more casual, it's a little more personal, and you don't have the guy standing there. You don't have all the logistical complications of that. You don't have to train people to become those kinds of [stand-up] reporters. And so it actually feels more natural because it actually is more natural.

When you're working with reporters—they are print people—so they've also learned to write for documentary and for video, which is very different. It's many fewer words; it's trying to use as much of the organic material that you've collected in the field. It's the reverse of what they do as reporters. As reporters, they write the article, they put in a few sound bites [the quotations from their sources]. What we want to do is have the sound bites carry the piece and then use the reporter's narration to link things together. But, you've also got, in some cases, amazing writers, and so you have that voice. And when you have the great voice it's fabulous, even if there's not actually a lot of narration. There can be, depending on what the piece is, but you just have that sense of their storytelling, which is nice to have.

In "Class Dismissed in Swat Valley" [profiled in Chapter 1], Adam Ellick wrote that piece, wrote the narration. He's an unusual person where he started out as a print journalist. He came to us, and started learning video; he actually came to us in the video unit. Now he's a video journalist and a print journalist. He's gone to Pakistan and Afghanistan twice as a combined print and video journalist. He reports for the Foreign desk and reports for us. And that piece he wrote the article and he produced a video, which is a huge amount of work. But he's like the combo model, you know? The hybrid reporter.

When you've worked with the *Times* reporters and the editors, my favorite response is, "Actually the video was better than the article." Sometimes by the reporter! You've got the images. And if it's the right kind of piece, it can be better because you have something to look at. Not always. There's plenty of pieces that do not lend themselves to video, but when it is, it's the perfect thing.

TRAINING—BE A JOURNALIST FIRST

I think people should have a blended curriculum. In New York we work with Columbia, New York University, and City University New York. We work with them pretty closely; we have interns from those schools. It's hard, it's challenging to learn how to be a journalist, and to learn how to shoot and learn how to edit, you maybe can't do everything, but to come out of journalism school now without some familiarity with video and/or audio and/or graphics—to have another language besides words I think is important. The thing I also know is we have these interns, they come, we adopt them. And a lot of them got jobs, and they've gotten jobs for organizations that are starting a video unit in journalism. They've gotten good jobs, and they've gotten good jobs because they've had multiple skills.

But the most important skill is that they're good journalists. You can get better at being a better shooter, a better editor, but the primary thing, which Adam [Ellick] had. When Adam came here he did not know how to run a camera, but he's a really good journalist. He already had a lot of experience, he has really good journalistic instincts, he works really hard, and then he taught himself everything else, or we worked to teach him.

What I get a fair amount of is [from potential interns and job applicants], "Well, I know how to shoot and edit." I'm like, "You know what? That doesn't do anything for me." You need to know how to be a journalist who knows how to shoot and edit. And I'd take the journalism skill over the [technical skill]—as long as you can turn on a camera and have rudimentary editing skills, that's good enough, because I can teach you that. But it's hard if you don't have the basic journalism skills and/or the instincts. And it's not all just skills, it's also just the willingness—that curiosity, the willingness to work hard that is like this engagement with the world that I think marks a good journalist. And that you have or you don't have, or you develop it or you don't develop it.

Video journalists have the hardest jobs in the world. They report, they produce, they write, they shoot, and they edit. On a big story—we like to team them up together. Sometimes we double team. That's actually really good, but it's really good when they have all the skill sets, especially if you have a longer project where you've got people moving—say they're working a couple different things at one time. When a shoot comes up and if one person edits and one person shoots, and if it's the day the editor's free, and you need shooting done, then you don't have any flexibility, so they all do everything. It's amazing, actually. And the standards are high, because we all [come from] broadcast television documentaries. It's not like, "It's just not good enough." It has to be on a tripod. The quality standards are really high—no shaky cam, no bad audio mixing, no camera mic—just nothing like that.

CHAPTER 4

Conducting Interviews and Writing a Script

A Workshop with "Icarus Refried: A Pro-Creative Process"

INTRODUCTION TO CREATING A SCRIPT FROM INTERVIEWS

To reiterate the importance of finding and creating story structure from your shots and interview material, I'll include my process in creating the nine-minute short documentary, "Icarus Refried: A Pro-Creative Process" (http://vimeo.com/24299832).

In this documentary on a performance artwork presented at the Clifford White Theatre at Northern Arizona University on April 26 and 27, 2011, I interviewed the two performers—one a clarinetist, the other a dancer and choreographer, on camera before the performance. I shot them individually. In addition, I shot some rehearsal footage and one night of the performance. A few days after the performance, I shot an interview of both of them together.

HOW TO CONDUCT AN INTERVIEW

I tell my students it's like going on a date—you want to show your subject respect, build trust, and get personal. You're there to help them tell their story, and this usually requires a heartfelt connection. Questions trigger emotional responses, so crafting the right questions is important, but listening for the subtext—the underlying emotional currents of your subject—is even more important. That's where the story lies—the emotional connection containing universal themes your audience will connect with.

Below, I include a transcript of the interview I conducted with John Masserini for my short documentary, "Icarus Refried: A Pro-Creative Process."[6] I'll include comments in brackets to reveal my thought process. In addition, I highlight the sections that I ended up using in the script.

Kurt: OK, so.
John: I look at you, not the camera, correct?

Kurt: So you play the clarinet, you're a master clarinet player. . . .

[I want to make the intro easy, something that I know the character is passionate about. Other than some email contact, I have not previously met John.]

John: I don't know if one would say a master clarinet player, but my doctorate is in clarinet performance. [Laughs.]

Kurt: What was your, was the clarinet your first instrument?

[Again, following it up with a logical, easy question helps me to discover his lines of passion. Even though it's a yes-no type question, it helps ease me into the next question.]

John: Yes.

Kurt: When did you realize you first wanted to play the clarinet?

[I'm trying to find the roots for his passion, material that a wider audience can connect with—it may confirm a pattern that they themselves have followed or they may see this person as someone they admire.]

John: I was ten years old and in the fifth grade. We were allowed to join band as an elective and I called my grandfather who was an amateur bassoonist and played in civic orchestras. I told him I wanted to play the piano and mentioned the piano is not such a great choice because you can't carry it around with you. I said "Okay," hung up the phone, and picked up a clarinet. That's the end of it. I've been playing the clarinet for twenty-eight years.

[In the back of my mind I know that this is good stuff—a story that an audience will find interesting and I'll use it in the script.]

Kurt: Were there other instruments you learned?

[This is a filler question as a way to get further background factual info.]

John: For a music degree typically you have to be proficient on piano, have to be able to sing, stuff like that. I was a saxophonist as well, and when I was at Idaho State University I was the saxophone professor for several years. But clarinet was my primary instrument all the way through.

Kurt: So, were you classically trained?

John: Yes, I was completely classically trained, no jazz, none of it—just strictly classical. I believe one genre is hard enough to learn. [Laughs.]
        Jazz is a completely different animal; as is Klezmer; as is East Indian clarinet playing. There are lots of different types of clarinet playing.

Kurt: Are the pieces from your performance improvised?

John: No, these are all composed pieces. Joan Tower's "Wings" which is a pinnacle piece in the clarinet repertoire. The third movement of Messiaen's "Quartet for the End of Time" which is just a solo clarinet piece. Another work in which we used a Robert Cogan score; he is a composer at the New England Conservatory. It is an aleatoric composition. He gives the clarinetist a thick folio of musical material, split up in the segments and fragments. It is the performer's responsibility to choose a certain number of segments within a certain number of fragments and there are just general rules on how many times you can repeat material. It is entirely up to the performers to decide the order, length, duration, everything. This intrigued us so we sat down one summer with the entire folio, I played through everything, and we discovered what we wanted. In one of the interludes of the evening I'm also performing a tiny one-minute snippet from a work by a composer I did my dissertation on, Eric Mandat. He is an avant-garde clarinetist and composer who lives in Illinois. Brilliant player. Brilliant composer. So I'm glad that if it is only for a minute that I get to pull some of his music in which I have a strong affinity for as well.

[This is a long answer and John provides a lot of detailed information—factual material that I may need for the story. It provides me material about the composers that I don't know anything about and it may reveal reasons about his choices that could be of interest to an audience for the documentary.]

Kurt: How many pieces?

[This is my fact checking to make sure I'm aware of who and what each piece of music he plays in the work I'm doing a documentary about.]

John: Cogan, Tower, Messiaen, Mandat—so four. . . .
          I have a really strong connection with the Messiaen for some reason. He wrote it in 1942 when, I believe, he was in a prisoner of war camp in WWII. And the piece, the "Quartet for the End of Time" has a huge history behind it. It was premiered in a Nazi camp and it is written, for piano, clarinet, violin, cello.

[Bingo. This is a great answer that spontaneously came from him—after I had reinforced my earlier question about the number of works used. He begins to go into why he has passion for a particular composer. In the edit I don't use all of this highlighted material, editing out sections of it so as to maintain a smoother flow in the rhythm of the edit.]

Kurt: Where do you perform it?
John: That's the scene with the eggs. That's called a piece we call "Shattered Flight" and actually what is interesting is Joan Tower's "Wings" is inspired by Messiaen. So I wanted to make that reference but there is something about that piece that really speaks to me in terms of color sound and emotion. I really love that piece. I learned it when I was twenty years old and it is one of those things I come back to every three to four years and I find a whole new layer to it. It is only five minutes long and it isn't all that difficult to play technically, but to get that emotional content it requires a certain amount of maturity that I know I didn't have when I was twenty and now I find it is getting deeper and deeper as I perform it.

[John reveals an emotional connection to the work that goes back to when he was young, starting out as a musician. I don't use the full quote in the final work, but the essence of the answer is the rich emotional connection he talks about. That emotional connection is a larger theme that can connect with an audience as it relates to how an artist develops their vision over time and, when they change and grow, their approach evolves. The universal theme an audience can relate to is change.]

Kurt: What is that process?

John: [Working with Melanie,] I feel we have a marriage, a creative marriage; we can say anything to each other. But this is where we differ in our relationship: I tend to treat things so "sacred," so to me the Messiaen was going to be about death, darkness, and seriousness. I wanted it to be emotionally overwhelming to the audience, I was not going to move too much because I want all the light and color to do this. Of course, I am not thinking theatrically, I'm thinking musically, and this is where our relationship has made me a completely different artist. You know I say this to everyone, I don't think I've even said it to Melanie, but I'm a completely different musician and artist because of her. I would not be anywhere near the kind of musician that I am today, much less an artist, if it wasn't for Melanie Kloetzel. She has completely changed me.

[This answer is great, because it speaks to John's working relationship with Melanie, but I only use the last bit of it because a later answer he provides says the same thing more passionately and succinctly. And I use this snippet as a good transition piece in the script.]

John: We talked to each other six, seven years ago, and decided we'd like to work together. I walked into the studio with my music stand and my clarinet and I put it down on the floor and I said "You go dance and I'll play." And Melanie said "No, that is not collaboration. You come out here with me." I said, "No, I'm the musician, I stand here and play and you dance and we're done." That was the beginning. As we worked with each other, I finally realized what it was to truly collaborate, to truly interact and to be multi-disciplinary to work within each other's medium.

[This is perfect for the story structure—we get a change in character here. John has changed how he collaborates with Melanie and it shows the type of character he is. He has the humility to evolve his artistic work by taking risks.]

John: What has happened now is that I am getting away from the music more and more and more. Even in our 2009 performance I still had a few music stands on stage because there are so many notes and there is so much to memorize. But we got to a point where we felt like we can't go any further with these pieces until I get rid of the music.

I finally made the decision that I'm going to memorize everything I play, no matter what. That process has really pushed me, challenged me, and now the interaction of the movement with the performing of the music gives it an entirely new direction and depth.

We still compromise. There are still parts where the music is really technically difficult, and I would prefer not to move. Sometimes the piece requires very little to no movement; it is nice to stand still now and then.

[This is good material, but I can't fit it in this short documentary.]

Kurt: What do you mean?

John: It's about embodying the works. I talk about this with my students all the time. You have to embody how to play the clarinet before the music can come out. If you don't feel comfortable playing the instrument, the music is never going to reach a higher level. And for us to work together this way and create these types of pieces, I have to fully embody them. It is not just notes, but it is also motion, and music making, and then the relationship between Melanie and I. We have to connect.

[If I was doing a longer piece on the process, showing more of the rehearsal and how he embodies it, I would use this material, because it's strong.]

Kurt: How was it like to collaborate in the beginning?
John: It was very scary in the beginning. I was really . . . it was scary. But actually what I find is that when I do traditional performance now, stand there and play by a music stand, it is so much easier; I'm not dancing around stage while I am performing. I can just stand here and play. So it has made [doing those kinds of performances] easier, but in the beginning it was scary. It had a lot to do with trust. I trust Melanie one hundred percent. She is amazing not only as a performer, but as a scholar as well. She is an amazing pedagogue, and she knew what my limits were. So in the beginning she had to teach me. And I read a lot. I read a lot about modern and postmodern theory, which was great because I'm intellectually curious about that.

    Again, she knew what my limits were, so she knew when I was starting to get really distressed she would say "Okay we can stop here" or "Let's modify it". But she knew if I said, "Yeah, I think I can" she would push me a bit further. So now it is not a big deal.

[This is good, rich material and, if I were to shape the story around their collaboration, I would use it. My story is broader, wanting to get into the meaning of the work, and have some material about the importance of the collaboration and trust.]

Kurt: Give me an example of how you engaged theory.
John: Yeah. In the beginning I was trying to make everything serious or pretty. And the models in my mind were always the modernists, the Martha Grahams and those artists. I love John Cage and I saw this documentary on John Cage: *I Have Nothing to Say and I'm Saying It.* In this film, it explored his relationship with Merce Cunningham and the use of chance convergences. It started opening up my brain to this idea that it doesn't have to look a certain [classical] way. This is the relationship. This is the art work.

    When we were in Calgary a month ago, and Melanie and I went to a dance performance. While we were walking home and I said, "I feel sort of bad" and she said, "Why?" And I said, "Because I don't look beautiful like that on stage, I am not a beautiful dancer." And Melanie just looked at me like "Silly child. If I wanted to work with dancers I'd work with dancers. I work with you and this is our art."

    I tend to slip into that mentality often. I think I need to look better; I need to look like a dancer. And the very opening scene of Icarus where we walk on the diagonal, and we get about here [gestures with hands]. The whole time we're looking at each other and it's sort of like . . . I see in Melanie's eyes, "You're going to do it, we're going to do it, you're good, we're good." I just need that little bit of reassurance and then from there that sort of opening connection really makes me really happy.

It's just, it's love. It's just, I mean I love her so much and she loves me. We wouldn't be doing this for so long if we didn't love each other, if we didn't want to create, work together.

While I was working here [in Flagstaff] before she got here [for the rehearsals] she was in her finals in Calgary and I was in space by myself for a whole week every night. I would run stuff, and it was fine but it wasn't good and was hard, and I talked to her on the phone. She said, "You know once I get there it is going to be better." And she is right. My favorite moments are when we are warming up. She'll be warming up but we're sharing the space together.

Kurt: Fantastic. Thank you.

John: You know you can always come back and ask me more if you want.

The interview lasted about fifteen minutes, but I got a lot of good material in a short time. It's important to get the subject to talk, and you must relate to the person—be interested in them and what they have to say, otherwise you won't likely get what you need to shape your story. I have an interest in the performing arts, so I might not know anything about this particular piece other than reading a couple of reviews during my research, but I have a passion for the topic and I try to infuse my questions with that passion so the subject sees me interested in what's being discussed.

In the end, it's about engaging in a conversation, discovering who the other person is, what their passions are, and helping them open up and share personal stories. This takes a certain amount of trust, because as the journalist you will be sharing their story with an audience and you need to be fair and accurate. They're opening up their heart, trusting you in translating their story to the world.

For this particular story on this performance, I then conducted an interview with Melanie. Both of these were done before the performance. I also observed a rehearsal and saw their collaboration at work. I could have used this footage in the work, but decided against it, since I chose not to craft a story about how the piece was put together. I wanted to tell a story about how they're passionate about their art, what that art means to them, and how their collaboration is a form of artistic passion and love. A few days after the performance, I met up with both of them and did a two-person interview on camera.

If I were to take all of the interviews and put it together as a documentary, I would lose the audience. It would be slow, ponderous, and lack meaning as a whole. Despite the fact I made connections with them during the interviews, showing an interview without any kind of editorial—storytelling filter—would cause the work to fail. It is your job as the video journalist to shape the raw material into a compelling story. And the easiest way I know how to do this is to craft a script from interviews.

Below, I show how I took the interviews and turned it into a script.

HOW TO TRANSFORM A TRANSCRIPT INTO A SCRIPT

After the shoot and the final interview, I processed the video files and exported them as audio files and hired someone to transcribe them, comprising about sixteen pages of material. Spreading the pages out, I went through them, circling material I thought was strong, putting numbers beside each in the order I wanted the story to flow from beginning, middle, to end. In essence putting together a paper edit. I then opened up a freeware script layout software package, Celtx.com, and copied and pasted the material.

Below, I provide a single-column reproduction of this script. I break the script into story structure sections: Hook and set-up, complications and conflict, climax and resolution. The numbers before the dialogue refer to the number I circled in the transcripts. At the time I was writing the script, I knew in general what images from the performance I wanted, so I didn't describe them in detail, but, as I was editing, I would find the most compelling images that fit what the performer was saying in the interview. Much of the dialogue went beneath the performance visuals, so you can hear the subject speak as we see the scene they're talking about unfold onscreen.

The words of the subjects' voices became the means by which I shaped the structure of the story. No narration was needed, since their words provided enough information to stand on its own. As for the images, if I had just got a wide shot of the stage for the entire performance, it is unlikely I would have made the documentary. The fact that I shot medium and close, as well as wide, allowed me to put the viewer into the performance by getting close enough to see the emotional expressions of the performers. In other words, the visuals supported the story, allowing the audience to enter the world of the performance through the emotional shots. The dialogue of the subjects offers context.

CASE STUDY—AN ANALYSIS OF THE SCRIPT FOR "ICARUS REFRIED: A PRO-CREATIVE PROCESS"

The completed documentary is not a literal presentation of this script, but a paper edit, the tool I used to get to the rough cut. As I played scenes, I shifted some material around, cut some, and added other shots and dialogue. So if you watch the documentary online, it doesn't exactly follow the script below. I provide the script with my comments in brackets explaining some of the choices made.

Icarus Refried: A Pro-Creative Process
by
Kurt Lancaster

HOOK AND INTRO:
John performing on stage, interacting with Melanie.

JOHN

1)   I was ten years old and in the fifth grade. We were allowed to join band as an elective and I called my grandfather who was an amateur bassoonist and played in civic orchestras. I told him I wanted to play the piano and mentioned the piano is not such a great choice because you can't carry it around with you. I said "Okay," hung up the phone, and picked up a clarinet.

[In the completed documentary, we see John slide in on the floor and pick up his clarinet, playing it. Melanie enters and jumps on his back at the end of this sequence. His words beneath this action provides a nice counterpoint to a story in which we think we may only be seeing a story about a clarinetist. The visuals tell us that he isn't your typical clarinet player.]

Head shot of John.

[The head shot allows us to see him first time, providing a release to what we've just seen.]

JOHN (CONT.)

That's the end of it. I've been playing the clarinet for twenty-eight years.

Shot of Melanie performing.

MELANIE

2)   It was not until I started exploring the dance scene that I started to get a lot more excited about it and . . .

Head shot of Melanie.

[This section allows us to be introduced to Melanie and the reason behind what drives her to dance. It offers a parallel structure to John's story.]

MELANIE (CONT.)

. . . there was something about bringing the physical body, in all aspects and in all kinds of variations, to the stage that was really intriguing to me.

Shot of Melanie and John performing.

[The following material from John provides us with the central conflict or question— why does he perform a clarinet on stage like this? It helps shape his identity and makes his work unique.]

JOHN

3)   I am not the worst clarinetist in the world, but I am certainly not the best clarinetist in the world. Quite frankly, I don't need to play the Brahms sonata in recital anymore.

Head shot of John.

JOHN (CONT.)

I feel that I'm not going to be the kind of clarinetist where people are going to pay money to come and hear me play a Brahms sonata or really standard repertoire, necessarily.

John and Melanie performing on stage.

JOHN (CONT.)

This is something unique. This is how I can make my stamp in the clarinet world. It is not playing Brahms; I'll leave that for the more famous people. But this is something that is unique to me and I'd like to maximize, take that further.

Head shot of Melanie.

[Melanie's words below link us to John's story and how the process makes her express her work uniquely in a collaborative way.]

MELANIE

4)   I really have to listen in a completely different way and we have to create something together that makes sense for both of us on stage.

Head shot of John.

JOHN

5)   I'm a completely different musician and artist because of her.

John playing clarinet as dialog on stage with Melanie reacting.

[I link the above idea of collaboration from what Melanie has just said to how John perceived how they first collaborated with the story below—which is a lot different from how he ended up collaborating with Melanie.]

JOHN

6)   We talked to each other six, seven years ago, and decided we'd like to work together. I walked into the studio with my music stand and my clarinet and I put it down on the floor and I said "You go dance and I'll play."

Head shot of John.

JOHN (CONT.)

And Melanie said "No, that is not collaboration. You come out here with me." I said, "No, I'm the musician, I stand here and play and you dance and we're done." That was the beginning. As we worked with each other, I finally realized what it was to truly collaborate, to truly interact and to be multi-disciplinary to work within each other's medium.

[The hook and introduction are complete. We get the sense of who these characters are and why they do what they do. In the conflict or rising-action section, we begin to dig deeper into Melanie's thinking process about a section of the performance I call chickens. She dresses up as a chicken and then the performance evolves into a scene of sexual subtext as she discusses the notion of procreation as "an aging academic female." The explanation and work become personal and I chose to use this moment in the documentary because of her raw honesty, as well as the strong images tied to this particular scene in the performance.]

RISING ACTION—CHICKENS

Scene from chicken in tub.

[For this script, I'm using scene notes as a reference; referring to the scene from chicken in tub is a key phrase that allows me to know what visual I want to use when editing. The visual was already shot before I wrote the script, so I'm not being precise in the description of these visuals, since I'm the one editing the material from what I've shot. If I were to hand the project off to someone else to edit, then I would have gone through the footage and described the precise moment with the listed time code. This particular visual moment has to be humorous since she is discussing how she likes to communicate humor to an audience. I choose the shot where she picks up a plastic egg and cracks it open to reveal a marshmallow chicken peep, which she eats.]

MELANIE

7) I really like how I can communicate certain types of humor in particular to an audience . . .

Head shot of Melanie.

MELANIE

8) . . . so they don't necessarily have to be on stage participating in it but that the performance is bringing them to those humorous places.

Scene from chicken in tub, later with recipe/banana.

[For the explanation Melanie provides below, I chose a few seconds of her performing the reading of a banana custard recipe, expressing sexual subtext as she does so. At the same time, we see a projection of a performer eating a banana in a sexually suggestive way.]

MELANIE

9) The character is really odd from the beginning, right? You can tell it's obviously representing a chicken, but then this chicken is getting extremely sexual in the end part of the piece, and then you see this "being" back stage or on the film projection eating bananas and being also relatively suggestive with the banana.

Head shot of Melanie.

MELANIE (CONT.)

Is she really doing that? [Laughs.] I love that question, "Is she really doing that?" because, you know, that surprise element is really fun. I mean I think people appreciate surprises in everyday life and in the performance setting it just, it definitely feeds me as a performer.

Scene with John and Melanie interacting, sexual tension.

MELANIE

10) So the chicken came out kind of right away. And then the sexually suggestive aspects of it really brought up notions of eggs and as an aging academic female there is always a certain like . . .

Head shot of Melanie.

MELANIE (CONT.)

. . . Oh, your biological clock is happening and what is that going to mean for you in terms of your profession?

[The performance is risqué in the above section, and I may not have included it in the documentary, if I didn't have her explanation—the deeper pro-creative meaning for Melanie's desire to put the material in the work in the first place.]

End of scene with John and Melanie interacting, sexual subtext with Melanie at end, picking her nails.

[In my final edit, I cut the section below, since it wasn't really needed for the final story. The high point was the previous scene. This material below became extraneous.]

MELANIE

11) But, at the end of the piece, this very postmodern comment of, "You know what I'm over this," where I just stand there and pick my nails then walk off stage. That kind

of quick change (snaps fingers) is one of those moments that the audience wonders, "What, did she just pick her nails on stage? Does she know that she is still on stage?" That feeling is really fun for me.

Head shot of Melanie.

MELANIE

12) It's also interesting from the perspective of John being a gay man who is not interested in reproduction in that particular way and/or the egg, perhaps, and so there is kind of a rejection on his part of it.

[This is a strong reveal about John and originally, as noted below in the script, I wanted this moment tied to rehearsal footage.]

Rehearsal shot of John and Melanie with John saying he doesn't want to be touched in this way (her hand sliding up his leg).

[However, the audio was low and visually it was the only shot from the rehearsal in the piece, so it didn't feel right. I ended up using the moment from the performance where her hand slides up his leg, without his rehearsal commentary. In the following section, I focus on John's solo piece, as a counterpoint to Melanie's solo performance we just discussed. For him, in his interview he discusses the importance of this particular song for him, so I include several shots from this solo sequence as he talks about it.]

RISING ACTION—EGGS

Scene with John performing clarinet solo with eggs.

JOHN

13) There is something about that piece that really speaks to me in terms of color sound and emotion. I really love that piece. I learned it when I was twenty years old and it is one of those things I come back to every three to four years and I find a whole new layer to it. It is only five minutes long and it isn't all that difficult to play technically, but to get that emotional content it requires a certain amount of maturity that I know it didn't have when I was twenty and now I find it is getting deeper and deeper as I perform it.

[To transition to the climax and resolution, I found a moment in the transcript where Melanie discusses how their process is getting deeper and deeper and what that means to her. This was a great moment to come out of John's words where he explains how he feels this piece of music gets deeper and deeper for him. Find moments in your transcripts where you can link the words. If you can't or if you need to write a narration to provide context, use the words of your subject to help you transition into the next section.]

CLIMAX AND RESOLUTION

Head shot of Melanie.

MELANIE

14) We feel like we are just going deeper and deeper and deeper. It's not just that you discover something about the person you are working with, because you absolutely do, and you discover something about the relationship, which you absolutely do, but you are discovering the degree to which you can take your form.

Head shot of John.

JOHN

15) When we were in Calgary a month ago, and Melanie and I went to a dance performance. While we were walking home and I said, "I feel sort of bad" and she said, "Why?" And I said, "Because I don't look beautiful like that on stage, I am not a beautiful dancer." And Melanie just looked at me like "silly child." And she said, "If I wanted to work with dancers I'd work with dancers. I'm working with you."

[When I read the above story by John in the transcript, I knew I wanted it at the end of the piece. It set up the strong creative and working relationship between the two performers.]

Opening scene of Melanie and John crossing on stage.

JOHN (CONT.)

And the very opening scene of Icarus where we walk on the diagonal, and we get about here (gestures with hands). The whole time we're looking at each other and it's sort of like . . . I see in Melanie's eyes, "You're going to do it, we're going to do it, you're good, we're good." I just need that little bit of reassurance and then from there that sort of opening connection really makes me really happy.

Head shot of John

[Below, when John says that they have this love for each other, that's the emotional release, the climactic moment that brings the story together. Up to this point, we're introduced to the characters—perhaps we feel the work is a bit strange, outside our typical understanding of a live performance (not quite a music concert, not quite a theatrical play)—but something different, a performance art work, perhaps challenging not only our visual sense of what gets performed on stage, but challenging our notions of how a musician performs on stage with a dancer, as well as the emotional tension and connection between the two performers on stage. The work with the chicken and banana sexual subtext also may challenge our notions of reserve in live performance. But the work clarifies itself and the documentary makes clear the deeper meaning behind the work—the tight creative relationship between two different kinds of artists. The declaration of Platonic love from John becomes the resolution, followed by Melanie's explanation of asking herself "Was all the hard work worth it?" And she provides the answer about the journey of herself, John, and the audience as the reward for the work.]

JOHN (CONT.)

It's just, it's love. It's just, I mean I love her so much and she loves me. We wouldn't be doing this for so long if we didn't love each other, if we didn't want to create work together.

Head shot of Melanie

MELANIE

16) During the week, I was like, "God, this is just so hard, why do I do this?" And then you get to the end of the performance, right, and you realize we were able to take ourselves somewhere, we were able to take the audience somewhere, somewhere that was not expected. Those elements, I mean, they're priceless.

This text became my paper edit to an actual rough cut. I discovered that it was easier for me to create a strong rough cut by writing a script first. It made the process quicker and forced me to think about the story structure first, rather than wading through all the shots and scrubbing through interviews, trying to find the best material haphazardly. In the past, I would wing it, finding key moments intuitively and it worked. It just took a longer amount of time. In the "Icarus Refried" documentary, no narration was needed, since I was able to find not only the contextual information, but the emotional moments within the subject's words. With the interviews transcribed, I could quickly go through the material and piece together the story structure from the emotional moments of what the characters were saying. It took less than a day to create the script and put together the rough cut.

WORKSHEET—EXERCISE 1

Record an interview and then transcribe it. Print it off and lay the pages out. Read through the material and start circling the most interesting material—the moments of emotion—and start putting these in order by putting numbers on them. You could also cut them and tape the pieces together to see the story flow.

If you're actually working on a short shooting assignment, then transcribe all of your interviews and create a paper edit from these interviews, taking note of any strong visuals you've already shot that can match the words being spoken. If you're missing images, then go back and shoot more. Make sure the work has a tight story as drawn from the words of your subjects, but also make sure you express that story visually through your shots. If you have more than 10 to 20 percent of a talking head, then the work will lack the documentary style you're looking for—shoot a lot of action shots in order to maintain strong visual journalism.

SCRIPT WORKSHEET

By doing the worksheet, you will set yourself up for a paper edit that will help you quickly achieve a rough cut.

- ✧ Transcribe your interviews and print them off.
- ✧ Describe what occurs in your action shots.
- ✧ Read through the transcripts and circle decisive moments—emotional high points that stand out to you. Take note of particular shots that will support the interviews.
- ✧ Arrange these into the following story structure elements:
  - – Hook
  - – Set-up, introduction
  - – Complications, rising action, conflict 1, 2, 3, . . . (there should be several)

- – Climax, crisis point
- – Resolution.

✧ Copy and paste these into a script-formatting software package.

FOR FURTHER READING

Hampe, Barry. *Making Documentary Films and Videos*. Holt Paperbacks, 2007. A great book on explaining the stages of writing multiple drafts of documentary scripts.

Interlude

The Most Important Journalists—From an Interview with Jimmy Orr, Managing Editor, Online, the Los Angeles Times

I think there's a big place for video. We know the power of text right now, and the text is what's working, and so how can we, with our resources, also produce video as well? Everything costs something. So if you have a finite number of resources, where do you put the bulk of the resources? Right now it's text. Is video important? It's really important. So do we produce video? Do we outsource for it? Is there a combo? I think there's probably some kind of a combo. And there's a lot of personal initiative, too. People are in control of their own destinies in journalism, I believe. And it's up to the reporters who want to get ahead, that want to say, "I want to lead." They're going to do more. They're going to write more, they're going to do their own videos, they're going to participate in podcasts, they're going to communicate with other journalists. It's the ones that have the initiative that are going to be the leaders. I think the model is changing and those that are really ambitious are going to be the ones that find the way, and they're going to also be the ones that are the most valuable.

Video multimedia tells a different part of the story. They can tell a more powerful part of the story. From a business perspective, it's important to keep people on your side as long as possible. It just is. Now, if you provide a video to augment a textual story, are people going to click on it? Quite oftentimes they do, and when they watch that video, are they apt to stay around longer? They are. So it's really important. It's important in telling a story, it can add a lot. It's also important because of the business need to have people stick around.

A unique video telling a story documentary style, that's where we're going to get the repeat traffic—if people like that, if they see something that is unique, that might not be nearly as professionally produced, but has that authenticity about it. If we have somebody who's over Pakistan telling a story, we're able to produce a video of that person's perspective, what they're saying, and talking to people. It takes you to that location and people are able to experience it differently. Again, I think it all goes back to unique content, and the power of unique content, and much like in texts and video as well, if we can provide something different, that's where the value is.

The more weapons one can have in their arsenal, the better, really. If reporters are able to communicate the news story in a minute and a half via audio, well there's value to that.

If they can stand in front of the camera and talk about the story, there's value in that. If they know how to interview and edit a piece together, there's a lot of value in that. Of course they know how to write. That's the foundation right there. And so the more that people can do all of those, the more valuable they'll be.

Again, I think that we see a lot of angst, and a lot of doom, and a lot of anxiety and wringing of hands, and I understand that, and I get that, because we're going through this tumultuous change, but we will find the way out. All that's changing is how frequently a newspaper gets updated. That's it. That's the only thing that's changing. We will have something we can hold. We're just going through a transition. Right now, you either have a newspaper itself, made out of a dead tree, or you have a computer monitor. And in the future, in a few years, we're going to be able to hold the monitor like we hold a newspaper. It's not delivered to your door, it's just updated online. And it will be frequently changing. That's the difference.

CHAPTER 5

Editing for Rhythm

Travis Fox's "Redefining China's Family: Women"

INTRODUCTION TO EDITING FOR RHYTHM[7]

Karen Pearlman, in her groundbreaking book *Cutting Rhythms* (Focal Press, 2009), posits how audiences must sync up with a film's rhythm—which is the editor's job of constructing a series of scenes that build tension and release in the audience. The core components of editing, Pearlman notes, include timing, pacing, and trajectory phrasing as a means to shape the three elements of rhythm: time, energy, and movement. Timing includes "When cuts and shots occur" (Pearlman 2009: 44), as well as which shot to choose, how long to stay on that shot, and where to cut (p. 47). Pacing shapes "the spectator's sensations of fast and slow" (p. 47). Trajectory phrasing sculpts the flow of energy from the movements within shots and from shot to shot—"the rise and fall over time of intensity of energy" (p. 58). When applied to the time-intensity story graph described in Chapter 2, we can begin to see how editing is a key component of structuring the hook, exposition, conflict, climax, and resolution of a story. If the climax of a story, for example, lacks energy in the edit, then the emotional intensity of the story itself will drag and lose its impact.

The editor, Pearlman notes, has at her disposal four different styles to engage an audience:

- montage
- decoupage
- collision
- linkage.

All of these are designed to help you think about how you shape the flow of energy during an edit.

Montage

Montage has several definitions, and Russian filmmaker and theorist Sergei Eisenstein discussed the theory of montage extensively, essentially requiring a process of making associations or an argument between unrelated images. Pearlman's definition entails a careful understanding of her other definitions, but relies on the weaving "together of images and sounds that are unrelated in time or space to create an impression, an idea, or an effect" (pp. 155–156). We see this style more often in documentaries than in fiction films. For example, in my documentary on people who want to go to Mars (http://redplanetdreams.com), the opening shot includes President Kennedy's Moon speech, with shots of Mars, and interviews with people who want to go to Mars. Because these shots all were independent of a single time and place, it's an example of a montage style of editing.

Decoupage

Decoupage, on the other hand, is the bringing together of similar images to create the illusion that everything is occurring in the same time and location. In Pearlman's words, it is "the cutting up of something that could unfold in real time and space into shots that will be put back together to create the impression of the events they contain unfolding in real time and space" (p. 156). This is the style we see in most films, and we see it in most of the examples found in this book.

Collision

The style of collision in editing refers to the weaving together of contrasting images in order to increase energy in a film, making it "feel more energetic, vibrant, angular, and aggressive" (Pearlman 2009: 162). These contrasts may include "image and sound, including light, movement, shape, direction, tone, shot size, focal length, contrast, dimensions, durations, speeds, performances, symbols, and so on" (p. 162). Similar to Block's principle of contrast and affinity in *The Visual Story*, the idea of contrast provides energy in a scene. Two shots of someone walking screen left to right followed by a shot of a car traveling left to right would be similar and convey less energy to the audience than a shot where the car moves from right to left—in contrast to the person walking from left to right. Oppositely placed images provide a sense of visual collision and increase energy.

Linkage

Linkage refers to the style that smoothly links shots together. "We are," Pearlman writes, "smoothly guided by the film's construction to empathy with characters and easy agreement with the ideas it contains" (2009: 165). Here the edits are smooth, with no abrupt changes, such as a dark tone shot followed by a bright one.

In most cases, the video journalist will feel their way through the editing process, letting instinct and story sense guide their style. But for video journalists who are editing pieces that are just not working, then the understanding of these different styles, the understanding of the function of editing as a means of creating tension and release in the audience, can help shape compelling videos that hook an audience. This tension and release is closely tied to the story structure.

THE EDIT IS THE FINAL DRAFT OF "WRITING"

Editing is key to telling stories in video journalism. It is the final draft of "writing" you'll do before the work is published. You become a better shooter when you master editing, since you only know what you need visually when you put together a story during the edit. The heart of good editing involves crafting moments of tension and release in the story.

How to Edit by Discovering What a Character Wants

The key to understanding how to edit revolves around determining what the central character wants and what he or she does to get it. Once you know what this is, then you can create a story structure that builds to the climactic point of the character attempting to get what they want or realizing that they're not going to get it. Or perhaps you withhold information after setting up a question and the climax is the reveal of this information. In my "Icarus Refried" documentary, the audience is presented with an opening shot of a clarinetist sliding in onto the stage floor, picking up his clarinet, and playing it, followed by a woman entering and jumping on his back. Who are these people? By the climax, it's revealed that the duo is creating a unique form of art from a deep love and respect for each other. In Travis Fox's "Crisis in Darfur Expands: Testimonials," he provides peaceful and pleasant shots of a refugee camp (children singing, goats walking by), then reveals the testimony of Abakr as she tells us her husband was killed—saving it for the climactic moment of this sequence.

Tip: Use Editing to Set up a Question, Then Answer It by Travis Fox

Fox utilizes editing as a form of setting up a "question and answer, so sometimes the video would pose a question, and the audio would answer it, or vice versa, so you would see a scene and it might spark some interest, and if you were like, 'Oh what's that?' And then the next frame answers it." At the same time, perhaps he'll focus on a particular shot, "if something's really tight, it's an interesting shot and then [the audience] may respond, 'Oh what is that? What is that sound?' and then you pull back and you say, 'Oh, I realize that's a turkey crossing the road,' or whatever it may be." Fox builds the structure in editing using the metaphor for building a house: "You build a foundation, you build up. So on the timeline, I do the audio first. And then I build up with [. . .] the best audio elements whether that's natural sound [or dialogue]. And then I get a proper sequence of those elements. And then write the narration in order to fill up that. And then I build the visuals last." As for the visuals, Fox says, "when doing the audio I kind of understand visually what the scenes are, and the sequence of the scenes, but still it's the audio that really drives the structure of the piece."

However, his work is not driven by audio narration, as typical in broadcast news pieces, but, rather, they're driven by interviews of his subjects and other natural sound elements. There is a conscious connection between the audio and visual. His narration is not personality-driven. It's functional, subservient to the story told by his subjects—and centered around his compelling visuals.

In any case, the character goes through an emotional shift at the climactic point—what Norman Hollyn calls the "lean forward moment"—the decisive moment where the story ups the ante. Once you discover this moment, you'll know how the story will resolve itself, so finding it is crucial for structuring a good story in the edit. If you can craft the emotional state of the character before and after the decisive moment, you'll have a clear beginning, middle, and end.

I've covered story development and character in Chapter 2. Also, I've shown some of the tools of cinematography (composition, lighting, camera movement) in Chapter 3. Furthermore, Chapter 4 covered how to develop a script from interviews, which helps you to structure your story and get you to a rough cut on paper. The editing stage allows you to bring it home—to take your material from a paper edit and place it on an editing timeline, which is the first place you can actually discover how the rhythm and pacing of the story flow feels. You may get a sense of it in a script, but you can't hone the ebb and flow of a story's energy until you edit.

To help with this process, the following outline will help you discover this in nearly any well-crafted story. This exercise is loosely drawn from Norman Hollyn's *The Lean Forward Moment* (2009). Before you edit your own story, nail down the **dramatic core of the story**:

1. Identify what the character(s) wants and what resistance he or she encounters. For example, in Travis Fox's "Redefining China's Family: Women," examined in this chapter's case study, we see the character of Wu, a single mother, attempting to exert her independence by purchasing her own condo.
2. How does the main character emotionally begin the story? She feels shame after her husband slept with another woman and told Wu to get out of the house.
3. How does this character emotionally end the story? She gains pride and freedom after she purchases her condo and tells her mother she is not going to try and save her marriage.
4. Where does that change happen? Identify this as the decisive moment. When she writes a check for the down payment.

Next, list all of your shots (size, camera movement, composition, actions occurring in the shot, audio, and duration of each shot)—this may be a lot of work, but it'll force you to think about the structure and flow of the story. Below, we will examine the story structure and shots in Fox's piece. With these shots, arrange them around the **decisive moment** in the **edit**:

1. Lay out the shots that occur during the decisive moment. Include the shot size, shot length, and audio.
2. Describe the action(s) occurring to invoke this change.
3. What happens in the shots before it? Include the shot sizes, shot duration, audio, and the screen direction of any action.
4. What happens in the shots following it? Include the shot sizes, shot duration, audio, and the screen direction of any action.
5. How can you shape an **audio design** that enhances the rhythm and pacing of the decisive moment? (Refer back to this after you read Chapter 6 on sound design.)
6. Can you build up to this climactic moment and fully resolve it?

Take note of the emotions you feel at this point—do you feel moments of **tension and release**? If so, then you're doing your job as an editor. If not, you may need to cut, trim, change up, or even shoot additional footage to make it work.

This level of analysis will help you think structurally about how to craft a solid story.

CASE STUDY: EDITING FOR RHYTHM IN TRAVIS FOX'S "REDEFINING CHINA'S FAMILY: WOMEN"

http://vimeo.com/1369597

Below, I provide the screen grabs from the first second of each shot in Fox's "Redefining China's Family: Women" from the *Washington Post* (2007). It is recommended that you watch the video online, before reading further.

Although this nearly seven-minute piece is heavily narrated by Fox, we can see how he uses visual and aural elements to structure the story itself, while the narration provides the audience with informational context. Fox utilizes all of these elements in his edit—crafting the rhythm of the story around a classic story structure model. Below, I provide the analysis within each piece of the story structure.

Hook—Shots 1–5 (0:00–0:20)

In the opening shot of this story about women in China, we see how Fox, hand-holding the camera, begins with a close-up of a telephone as we hear it ring, setting up the hook, a natural sound recording of a woman calling in to a help center. As the Chinese voice speaks, we see translated text appear onscreen as we cut to a woman's back in a small cubicle, a close-up profile shot of the woman on a phone, listening, and then a close-up of paper with a checklist. The shots present strong cinematography—even in such a stark functional space. Light falls across the bottom right edge of the telephone, providing a sense of depth and revealing the focus of the scene—a telephone conversation. The second shot presents a wider two-shot of the space, women working the phones in tiny cubicles. The woman on the left contains higher contrast—her black sweatshirt or jacket stands out against the brightly lit white cubicle, while the woman on the right is presented in more shadow, and she falls off on the right third of the screen. Because of Fox's composition and sense of lighting, we know visually that the woman on the left is the subject of the third shot, a side-view close-up of her on the phone counseling a distraught caller.

As these images place us in the counseling center, Fox presents a translation onscreen of what we hear in Chinese—the voice of a troubled woman speaking to the counselor on the phone: "When we fell in love, he treated me so well, but now he treats me worse than the people he hates"—the hook that pulls the audience into the story. When editing, Fox finds the best sound bites first, then he tends to script his narration around the sound bites, constructing his images around them. Even though the first ten seconds of the scene appear seamless, the images and audio were likely culled from ten to twenty minutes of footage, since Fox has a shooting ratio of at least ten to one. Each shot Fox chose during editing helps build a set of questions—where are we and what is going on?

Shots 1–5 The Hook. Travis Fox Opens with a Series of Close-ups as the Hook That Grabs the Audience.

Recreating pieces he shot during his visit, Fox uses the decoupage style of editing by linking the shots together seamlessly in order to answer those two questions visually and aurally. He shows us shots of a counseling center and we discover a woman sharing an intimate confession about her disintegrating relationship. These shots comprise the hook of the story and thematically set up the rest of the work, which tells a story of women asserting independence in a male-dominated, increasingly capitalistic China.

Tip: Dai Sugano Says to Find the Hook with "Wow, What's That?"

When Dai Sugano of *San Jose Mercury News* does his work as a video journalist, such as the poetic "Left Behind" (www.mercurynewsphoto.com/2008/leftbehind/), he still approaches his work as a journalist. He'll prepare and think about the images and questions he wants to get from an assignment. "I prepare and plan things in my head, that helps a bit. I'm going to shoot this way and ask this question. You interview someone or you see someone and it's more like editorial skills" when thinking about how to open a piece. "If you can acknowledge that this particular quote is very important, or this particular quote is very strong, it's the heart of your story, then you have it, then you have the opener. I look for those during the assignment. Somebody says something incredible. So for the intro, instead of introducing someone as, 'Hi my name is blah, blah, blah,'", Sugano rather "go[es] right to the great quote" (Sugano 2007).

We see this in Travis Fox's China piece on women, when we get that powerful sound bite: "When we fell in love, he treated me so well, but now he treats me worse than the people he hates."

Starting with an opening that may appear a bit confusing to the audience is okay, too, since Sugano wants the viewer to wonder what is going on—as long as the hook is strong. "It's okay to start with a little bit of unknown," Sugano notes. Perhaps the "viewer will say, 'Wow, what's that? What did he just say or what did she just say? That was cool, but I'm not sure where she's at or what she's doing.' And you see. You see in thirty seconds what she likes or what he likes." The audience isn't spoon-fed. Like a good film, he'll set up moments that require the audience to actively participate, while in the broadcast news style it's much easier to sit back and let the reporter—the host—do it for you—due to the narration telling the story.

Set-up, introduction—Shots 6–27 (00:21–01:55)

We are then led to the exposition, the explanation of what is going on with women in modern China. We see a cut to a wider shot of the confined space in the women's center as Fox narrates the location and how the center offers an insight into how the role of women is changing in China. This sets up the conflict and it will lead us to the main character who becomes representative of how one woman deals with her place in modern China. She doesn't appear until nearly two minutes into the film, but the hook and exposition set up the context to take us to her story. The exposition lasts about a minute and a half, comprising shots 6–27. For the first eleven shots of this section, we stay in the women's center, seeing shots of the counselors talking on the phone, listening, and taking notes.

Again, Fox utilizes decoupage and linkage as the dominant style in this piece. This sequence of shots visually forward the story of how these women work in the counseling center, a "hotline that provides support for women dealing with marital problems and domestic violence," Fox narrates. If the hook provides intensity, these shots shape a breather for the audience. It's a space for release—the editor's job is to build moments of tension and release

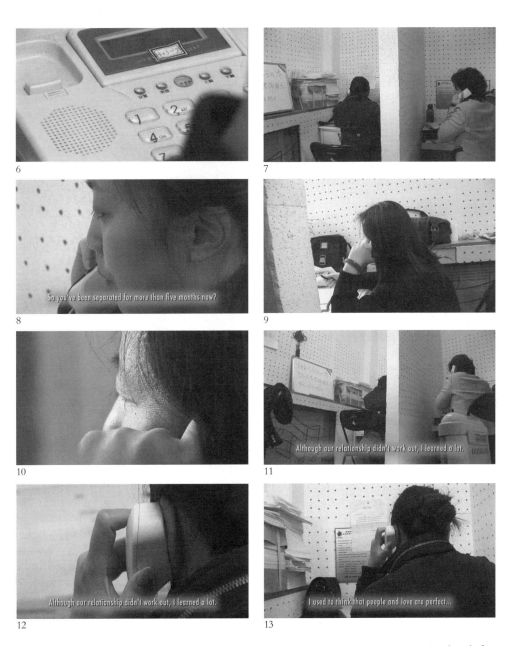

continued overleaf. . .

14   15

16

Shots 6–16 Setup and Introduction. Travis Fox utilizes the styles of decoupage and linkage.

throughout the story. And here Fox deftly crafts this moment as a way for him to not only provide emotional release for the audience, but also to give them the information needed to follow the story, contextualizing what's going on through his narration. He takes us in and out of moments of the women working the hotlines in order to help build more moments of minor tension, so as not to lull us into too much release through the narration. In shot 10, for example, Fox says that "traditionally these problems were kept quiet," followed immediately by shots 11–14, in which we see a low-angle back shot of two women on phones, and extreme close-ups of the telephone receiver pressed against the listener's ear and her writing notes with a pen. As we see these shots, we see this translation of a hotline caller: "Although our relationship didn't work out, I learned a lot. I used to think that people and love are perfect . . . but now I realize that we need to be practical."

It is this piece of information—the practicality in relationships—that sets up the rest of the exposition. We hear Xu Anqi talk underneath shots 15 and 16—we're still in the counseling center—but, through Fox's use of overlapping dialogue in editing, he smooths out the first moment of collision as we're taken through this transition into the professor's office at Shanghai Academy of Social Sciences as Xu Anqi provides scholarly context for the condition of women and relationships in China. We hear the voice of a translator: "We used to think about how others see us, and the reputation of our families. With people's changing ideas and less control in society, people are eager to look for happiness. Now they pay attention to love and quality of life." Notice that Fox doesn't tell us who Xu Anqi is through his narration. He lets us hear the translator's voice underneath shots 15 and 16, which poses the question, "Who is talking?" And then visually provides release through the answer in shot 17.

Fox lets her answer what the changing roles of women mean in society, then explains what that may mean on the streets of Shanghai, as he narrates the following:

Shot 17 Travis Fox cuts a rhythmic moment of release by cutting to the scholar Xu Anqi.

A growing number of women are seeking a better quality of life away from their husbands, sending China's divorce rates upwards. Although the rate here is less than half of what it is in the US, the number of divorces in China is skyrocketing. Divorces are up three-fold since the 1980s. In booming Shanghai, it's eight times that amount, and the signs of a new sense of individualism is everywhere—even in the music.

As Fox provides this narration, we're taken into the streets of Shanghai for ten shots (18–27), shots that visualize the themes of love, desire, and relationships—whether in advertisements for wedding rings, a portrait of a young girl smiling on the side of a building, or a song bursting out of a public speaker about women asserting their independence in the world of love: "I can only be single and I won't love anyone," the lyrics are translated on the bottom of the screen. The narration provides a key component of the linkage style. We're not disrupted from the story.

The song begins on shot 21, an advertisement for an engagement ring, right after Fox says, "The number of divorce rates in China is skyrocketing." He uses the sense of irony in his images to help propel the story through this section using montage—images taken out of one time and space in order to engage a dialectical argument about marriage, riches, and divorce in China. It develops the story—the giant building-sized image of a young girl slyly smiling down on us (shot 24)—an image that could have been in Ridley Scott's *Blade Runner* (1982)—as the song deepens the ironic sequence: "I can only be single and I won't love anyone." The beats of the song pull us through this exposition—which in the hands of a less-skilled editor might have lost the audience in a scene with too much release—but Fox provides tension through the ironic juxtaposition of images, narration, and music as he leads us energetically into the heart of the story.

At the same time, we see in this style of montage not collision, which takes us out of the scene, but linkage as Fox smoothly takes us into the streets of Shanghai as we come out of the scene with the professor in her university office. The shots of the people walking the streets, the advertisements, and the song seem to occur in the same time and place as Fox shot footage on the street. But, indeed, the shots were taken at different times and in different locations, but he links them all together, taking care not to jar the audience out of the narrative moment, the song providing the strongest link in shaping the energy in the rhythm at this point. Shots 23–27 strongly illustrate this. We see the wide shot and close-up of the girl image on the building, which is followed by shot 25, a close-up of a public speaker. We get the sense this song is coming through this speaker next to the large image of the sly girl,

Shots 18–27 Fox continues the setup and introduction by taking us into the streets of Shanghai for ten shots.

yet the shot, when examined closely, isn't near the picture. But through Fox's style of linkage in editing—he smooths over the disparity—and the montage (one shot, the girl, followed by a different shot, the speaker, both accompanied with the audio of the song) provides the audience with a sense of music coming from this location as if we're walking down the streets of Shanghai. And it works. But it could easily have failed if Fox didn't have a strong sense of the story he crafted from the images, narration, sound bites, and music.

Having no formal training in film editing, Fox instinctively engaged Pearlman's tools of editing: timing, pacing, and trajectory phrasing. He fades the music out over the next several shots, two of which takes us into a wide view of Shanghai (shots 26 and 27), the energy dissipating—another moment of release—as the music fades. However, at the same time, the energy shifts through these two cuts of the cityscape of Shanghai. The high-angle shot of the street (shot 27) contains a strong vertical with a Greek column steeple framed on the left third of the shot; the vertical and the trajectory phrasing between the cuts builds the energy to take us into the main conflict of the story.

Tip: Shape the Story through Key Sound Bites, Says Travis Fox

Fox tends to structure his pieces around the key sound bites. "You pull your best sounds, essentially," Fox explains. "So that can be quotes, that can be dialogue between subjects, and that can be found sound, wind blowing in the trees, that sort of thing. You pull those first, and that's what drives it." He'll then pull the audio elements he needs, skimming through the recording, and stringing them together on his editing timeline. "So, I have the audio, these are all the audio elements that I want to use at this point. There's two and a half minutes. I'd like to cut it down even more than that," he says as he points to his computer screen. He doesn't transcribe his interviews, either. However, he does skim through his shots and finds choice sound bites, the dialogue from his interviews that will catch the attention of the audience, and help structure the story—the emotional and information high points.

He then takes the choice sound bites and transcribes them. "I don't transcribe them word for word," Fox admits, "but just so I have a general idea so it can flow." That's the beginning of the script process. "So another twenty minutes and I'll get that done," Fox explains, "and then record the script, just with using the mic on the computer and do a rough edit with that, with the bad sound just so I can hear it and see if it makes sense, then I usually tweak the script, change things around, then I'll record it with a proper microphone, and replace [them with] the new clips in and be done with it."

Fox also brings together the other "audio elements, and then now I'm going to write the script, essentially. And then from there I will build in between the seams and build up on the visuals."

Conflict, Complications—Shots 28–48 (01:56–4:30)

The two wider shots of Shanghai shape the transition. The music begins to fade, and we are taken to city streets from out the side of a car, followed by shots of Wu Meifen, a young woman driving.

Shots 28–31 Conflict and complication 1. Wu Meifen represents the change in women's roles.

"Wu Meifen represents this change," we are told through Fox's narration. "She divorced her husband three years ago after he had an affair and did not try to hide it from her." She talks to Fox in the car as he films her, the visual action taking us somewhere. She conveys intent, which situates her character—one who has taken charge of her life after, as she says, "My ex-husband brought home a woman and slept with her in my bed. He told me to kill myself if I didn't like it. I don't think I'll ever forget the shame." Her story takes us through the next two shots of her driving (shots 30 and 31). Her discovery—the story she shares on camera—closes with a tight close-up, as we see how Fox records her determination. A key element of good cinematography captures honest moments of body language, revealing the underlying emotions of a character, which manifests the subtext, the dramatic need of the character. It becomes the catalyst for her life, and Fox, through good timing, takes us to the moment where she makes the most significant change in her life.

For this change, Fox narrates the steps she took that got her to this point. He uses a rearview shot of Wu holding her little daughter's hand as they walk towards a building (shot 32). Wu's daughter is prominently framed, and we see only the lower half of her mother. Fox follows as they walk, the energy in the shot propelling the story forward at Wu's pace. During this shot, we hear Fox narrate: "Wu was so humiliated, she says she left without taking anything except her daughter." This presents a moment of tension—supported by the energetic "trajectory phrasing" of the forward motion of the handheld camera following them. He ends the moment at a fountain, as we hear water providing a moment of release, the tension ebbing. Shot 34 reveals a front shot of the daughter talking to her mother—we don't know what she says in English, but Fox uses this moment to tell us about how Wu plans to overcome her humiliation: "First learn how to drive, then open a business, and eventually buy an apartment."

We don't see shots of her learning how to drive, but the opening of this sequence shows Wu driving—the shot provides visual evidence that she accomplished the first part of her plan towards liberation and independence. We don't see her working at her business and we're not told what that business is at this point. However, Fox does fortuitously take us on her journey the day she buys her apartment—the final fulfillment of her plan—and proof that she is earning money with her job. Without this sequence, the story wouldn't work nearly as well. We're presented with a strong central character doing something, the narration telling us just enough to get us to believe her capabilities as a character.

Here Fox presents a moment of tension as supported by the energetic "trajectory phrasing" of the forward motion of the handheld camera following Wu Meifen and her daughter. He ends the moment at a fountain, as we hear water providing a moment of release, the tension ebbing.

The camera in shot 34 pans right as Wu and her daughter walk past and they head towards the door of a large building. "After three years of living with relatives, her new life was about to begin," Fox tells us through his narration. We don't see her going through the doors, but Fox saves us the time—an editing ellipsis—by taking us immediately to a close-up inside, as she points to a model of her high-rise condo (shot 35). "The apartment I am buying is in the tallest building of the intersection," she points (shots 35 and 36). We're taken through a series of shots of the model utilizing different shot sizes and angles as Fox tells us how traditionally wives would stay with their husbands, no matter what. Even Wu's grandmother encouraged her to stay with her cheating husband in order to salvage the marriage (another source of conflict). Cinematically, Fox shoots a series of panning shots and a crane shot as he captures these emotional moments, providing visual elements that comprise the story of Wu as we see her overcome her past abuse from her husband—previously narrated by her—and take the final steps of liberation with her daughter by getting a condo on her own. The last image in this scene (shot 40), presents a crane-type shot starting high, then moving down to eye level of the model condo buildings. This creates the release, taking us out of the tension-creating news about her grandmother wanting Wu to stay with her husband.

32

33

34

Shots 32–34 Fox presents a moment of tension.

Cinematically, Fox shoots a series of panning shots and a crane shot as he captures the emotional moments of Wu Meifen overcoming her past shame.

She enters a world of masculinity and Fox's cinematography renders the emotional core of her story through the visuals of vertical sky rises (shot 36), and men consulting blueprints (shot 37). In shot 38, he provides a bird's eye view of the condo development model, before taking us to an interview of Wu, followed by the crane shot that takes us down to the model. This section provides the heart and space of Wu's independence—her dramatic goal of attaining freedom from the masculine dominance of her husband, and Fox's cinematic techniques visualize this desire with careful composition and lighting techniques. The editing shapes the energy in this scene and reinforces the style of decoupage with linkage throughout.

Shots 35–40 A series of panning shots and a crane shot.

The next eight shots (shots 41–48) show Wu with her daughter talking about their new place, as well as her meeting with a real estate agent or mortgage broker, as Wu writes a check—a down payment for her place. Fox even inserts a close-up (shot 42) of a coffee cup inscribed with "My perfect life"—a visual statement that not only provides a moment of release in the editing, but also thematically fits Wu's story, and the feminine change in China.

Fox then takes us to a key moment of the story (a decisive moment)—with shots and dialogue revealing Wu talking to her daughter about where they will soon be living. In shot 40, towards the end of the crane shot, we hear the daughter speak, with text translation onscreen, "It's on the 5th floor?" The overlapping dialogue takes us to shot 41, a two-shot of mother and daughter, as Wu explains, "The 19th floor, not the 5th." The daughter responds, "The 19th floor is high up." This moment shows the daughter moving her hand up high as

Shots 41–48 The dramatic need of Wu.

she faces her mother. The mother responds, "Very high," as the daughter shoots back, "That's a tall building." The interaction between the two reveals the daughter looking at the camera for a moment as the mother explains to her that, "Nearby there are playgrounds with slides where kids play." This kind of moment creates high energy as it reinforces a moment of sincere honesty and openness typically found in documentary films, and expresses a core component of what make documentaries powerful in a non-sensational way. It is a type of documentary vérité seen in a Maysles or Pennebaker film.

The rest of the sequence shows the action of Wu writing a check for the down payment of the apartment (shots 46–48)—this is the fulfillment of the dramatic need of Wu. She must attain her goal of gaining freedom, and we see her do it. The other moments from her life—as told through Fox's narration and her own voice—the discovery of her husband in bed with another woman, leaving home with only her daughter, moving in with relatives, learning to drive, and starting her own business comprise the backstory for this moment. Fox, giving us a piece of journalism, takes us through a snapshot of women in China calling into a crisis hotline center, talks about how women are gaining more independence, and presents Wu as a case study of the changing role of families in contemporary China.

These shots fulfill the dramatic need of Wu. She must attain her goal of gaining freedom, and we see her do it.

"Are you excited," Wu asks her daughter, the question reflecting her own goals being fulfilled and Fox captures the moment with emotional integrity. "Yeah!" she exclaims. We see shots of paperwork being filled out and the check signed, as Fox relates how the stigma of divorce is lessened due to the fact that women can become financially independent. It is only at this point that Fox reveals in the narration that Wu started her own tile business, earning enough to put 20 percent down on her condo. "Once the check clears, she'll get the keys to her new apartment. But she can't wait to check the progress of construction," Fox tells us as we see the signing of the paperwork and the handing off of the check. The screen cuts to black as we're taken to the climax of the story—the emotional highlight of Wu's life after hitting a low when she discovered her husband cheating on her. This is what she's been building for, the assertion of her own independence away from the control of men. And Fox's editing takes us on her journey.

Climax—Shots 49–52 (3:50–4:30)

The climax takes us to the unfinished stage of Wu's condo, a shot that reveals an empty space of concrete, drywall, and dirt on the floor. The camera pans around to Wu and her daughter in silhouette walking into the condo with sunlight shining bright through a window, the camera automatically adjusting for the lighting change, as the door opens, from black to bright sunlight coming through the window on the far wall. Wu, in silhouette, asks her daughter, "Are you happy" (shot 49), as she looks around the room. Her daughter says, "Look, look!" and she bounds offscreen into the other room. This is followed by one of the funniest moments in the piece, as Fox cuts to an extreme close-up (shot 50), of the daughter scraping her shoe in a pile of dust, imprinting a treadmark. Fox zooms the camera out to reveal a high-angle full shot, as she kicks the dust around. During this shot, we see Wu enter into the room and grab her daughter by the hand, pulling her away from the dirt. She looks up, smiling, "Look, that's my footprint!" He narrates: "Just like everything in China, divorce laws have changed rapidly.

Just four years ago, Wu would have needed permission from her employer to get a divorce, but since 2003, divorce takes just a matter of minutes." The section ends with a close-up shot of wires hanging out of a wall (shot 51), followed by a medium shot of Wu standing, facing the door (shot 52) as she says, "This is pretty good for a studio apartment. Well, for the two of us it will be enough." She looks back into the room and smiles. The daughter walks out of the room, followed by her mother. The scene fades to black.

The climax takes us to the unfinished stage of Wu's condo, a shot that reveals an empty space of concrete, drywall, and dirt on the floor.

What's of interest here is how Fox chooses the shots—the daughter kicking the dirt as the mother pulls her away. The narration juxtaposes this light moment with how easy it is to get a divorce, now, as opposed to the need to receive permission from a boss. The balance of information in the narration with the levity of the visuals helps us feel the climactic tone of the piece—Wu has attained victory, due not only to her tenacity and a willingness to become independent, but also from new laws that opened up the possibility for her, a possibility that might not have worked out if she had wanted to leave her husband a few years earlier. The smile she expresses as she looks back into the room is unstaged. It's a sincere moment of energetic release, an image that visualizes the climax to her story. In a typical story structure, this climax would be followed by a clear resolution, which we find beginning ninety seconds later in shots 70–78.

The next ninety seconds (shots 53–69) presents a detour—a "subplot" about a divorce counseling center. (I don't include the images here.) This side-story deflates the central narrative about Wu. Even though Fox spends nearly the first two minutes at a women's hotline center dealing with marital problems and abuse at the beginning of the piece, it helped thematically set up Wu's story—one about abuse—and it worked as a nice set-up to her story. However, this next section jars us out of Wu's narrative and actually breaks the dramatic flow. Indeed, the

49

50

51

52

Shots 49–52 Climax.

choice could perhaps have been made to either use the following section or the current opening as a way to introduce Wu's story. We've felt the build-up of tension leading us to the climax. But instead of a release through a resolution, the release takes us into another story—the resolution energetically deferred for us to discover later. Visually Fox takes us away from Wu's story by a fade-out to black and fade-in from black, as a way to ease us into this new section.

Side-Plot: Counseling Center—Shots 53–69 (4:31–6:01)

It begins with a close-up shot through a window of a skyscraper in the background. The camera pans around to reveal desks with people working in a counseling center dealing with divorces and relationship repair. After seeing Wu's arrival at her condo, we're expecting more about her story; we're sensing dramatically a need for a resolution. The end of the counseling center sequence talks about money and practicality being the basis of relationships—the idea is somewhat climactic, but visually it is not as compelling and we are no longer in Wu's story, on this woman's journey, so we don't feel it as strongly.

I think Fox may have included this section in the story because of the theme dealing with "love maintenance" and the booming business of divorce and counseling. The character in this section, Shu Xin, has a million registered users and thirty offices around China for his counseling center, Fox tells us in the narration. He offers advice and helps to save marriages, recommending divorces to only 20 percent of his clients. Thus the lessons learnt about women's role in relationships in the new China, resonates powerfully throughout the story, despite the side-bar feel to it. Fox sets up the piece with a quote from Shu (through the voice of a translator) that expresses his sense of humor (shot 54): "Our slogan is, getting divorce is worth celebrating because I don't have to listen to your scolding anymore. The second slogan: Getting a divorce is not going to change the status of my life. Third slogan: Divorce is not something we feel sorry for." Fox frames Shu, as he turns away from his computer and discusses these slogans. Fox then takes us out of this moment, by an even-level close shot of a phone ringing, before narrating about how Shu opened his business two years ago. He follows this with a tight shot of Shu discussing the success of the business, surpassing their expectations (shot 60). The style of linkage and decoupage remains.

He transitions us into the next section (shots 61–69), with a close shot of a sign that reads, "Divorce Research" (shot 61), and Shu asks his customer, "What kind of service would help you the most?" "Love maintenance," she replies. It's a funny moment, and, perhaps, worth the diversion from Wu's story. This half of the story shows Shu counseling a woman. Although not character-driven at this moment, the images are beautifully shot and this funny moment about "love maintenance" provides a release in the tension, but we've lost the narrative thread of Wu's story. This section is a fairly strong piece and acts as a juxtaposition to Wu's decision to get a divorce and not to follow her grandmother's advice. It's filled with Fox's signature visual and vocal style that unassumingly draws you into how he sees the world. Fox closes this section with a woman talking to Shu. She says, "I think money is the basis of relationships. Without money, there would be lots of fights. There's a saying that's very true at times . . . that relationships are based on money." A close-up of a building (shot 59), followed by a wider shot of a thrusting diagonal of the building lit in the sun (shot 60), energetically takes us out of Shu's story with a slow fade to black, and he brings us back to Wu, as Fox withholds her resolution up to this moment.

Resolution—Shots 70–78 (6:02–6:55)

The final shots of Fox's story, lasting under a minute, provide a strong resolution to the entire piece—the only stronger ending could have been to show Wu moving into her new apartment with her daughter, but, with a video journalist's limited time on the ground, this was an unlikely option. However, what Fox chooses to use as the ending resonates and encapsulates the changing role of women in China. Three of these shots are cutaways to a television show that Wu, her brother, and grandmother watch—it is a reality-based talk show dealing with, as Fox narrates, "love and divorce" (shots 70, 73, and 77). Structurally, it provides the thematic resonance for Wu's rationalization for striking out on her own, and it also provides a moment of closure for Wu's story. Fox chooses to use a moment from an earlier interview (shot 76), and we hear Wu through the voice of a translator say, "In the past, women were unhappy in marriages and they still chose to stay and therefore they suffered. Now we choose to exert ourselves. We take care of ourselves more. It's much better now." The close-up of the clock (shot 75) helps prevent the collision between seeing Wu on her couch to her in the interview. She is smiling, followed by a shot of the television as we see a couple walking away hand in hand (shot 77).

In the resolution, we see Wu spending her final nights at her grandmother's home. The television audio continues, as Fox closes (shot 78) wide with Wu sitting watching the television offscreen as her grandmother walks to a door and opens it. She steps in and closes the door. The scene fades to black. This ending is significant, since we discovered earlier that the grandmother was opposed to Wu's divorce and we hear through Fox's narration that Wu is spending her final nights here, before moving into her new place. The grandmother, perhaps holding to traditional ways, closes the door on her, refusing to interact on camera—a shot that encapsulates the shift from the old to the new role of women in China.

70

71

72

73

continued overleaf . . .

Shots 70–78 Resolution.

Tip: Story Structure is the Most Important Thing, Says Fox

Fox leaves us with some words of wisdom about how the story is more important than the quality of the video. He feels that those trained in photojournalism may "have some advantage in terms of composition and understanding light," but he feels that shooting video "is probably not the most important part." He admits that his "photojournalist colleagues would probably gasp at that, but," he adds, "the most important part is the producing, is the editing, is the story structure, is the narrative." At first he found this "the difficult part," which may be the case "for other photojournalists that are switching" to video. But he feels that, "You can have great images, you can have a series of great images, but if they don't edit together, and if you don't have a great story with a beginning, middle, and end, then it's not a good video." Conversely, you can have "mediocre photography" and if you have "an interesting story, great character, a good narrative arc," then you'll "have a perfectly good video." It works, because the story is what holds the audience to the video. "If you just have good pictures, and it's poorly edited, and there's no story, then that's not going to work," Fox contends.

And this is the key reason why Fox's videos are strong—the visual strengths enhance the strength of the story. "I think that even if it's a minute and a half or six minutes or ten minutes or twenty," Fox argues, "I feel like the structure is pretty similar. I go about editing them exactly the same. I'll pull the best quotes, arrange it, write the script and build it up, so whether it's a minute and a half or six it's the same way. They should have the same [story] structure."

Other than the side story, the energetic rhythm of the work flows nicely with conscious choices in the flow of emotional up and downs (tension and release) as it builds to a satisfactory climax and resolution. Fox took a story that could have been just about an overview of the changing role of women in China, and approached it as a documentary filmmaker—discovering the central issue, and placing the viewer into the world of one character, Wu, who becomes the personification of that issue, a character whose dramatic needs structure the overall story. Fox reveals the story through contextual narration, through the voice of those he interviewed, and shown through cinematography—the shots revealing the significant emotional moments that propel the story forward along classical lines of dramatic structure. We can plot the dramatic structure of Fox's story on a story graph, see Figure 5.1.

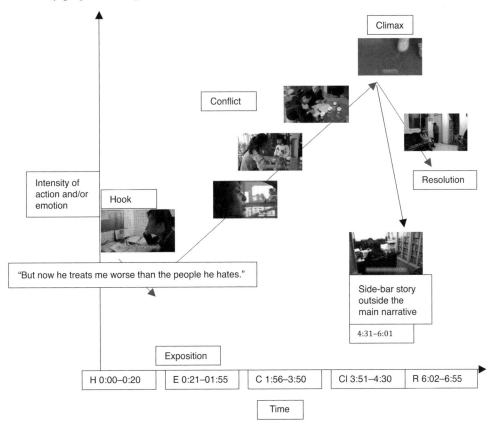

Figure 5.1 Story graph of Travis Fox's "Redefining China's Family: Women."

WORSHEET—EDITING ANALYSIS EXERCISE

A)   Analyze "Miracle on 22nd Street" on the *New York Times* (http://video.nytimes.com/video/
2010/12/24/nyregion/1248069482199/miracle-on-22nd-street.html) (or choose another
good piece of video journalism that you like).

1.   Describe the **dramatic core**:

a.   Describe each shot (size, camera movement, composition, actions occurring in
the shot, audio, and length of each shot).
b.   Identify what the character(s) wants and what resistance he or she encounters.
c.   How does the main character emotionally begin the scene?
d.   How does this character emotionally end the scene?
e.   Where does that change happen? Identify this as the decisive moment.

2.   Describe the **edit** (as it relates to rhythm and pacing):

a.   Describe what occurs in the editing during the decisive moment. Include the shot
size, shot length, and audio.
b.   Describe the action(s) occurring to evoke this change.
c.   What happens in the shot before it? Include the shot size, shot length, audio,
and the screen direction of any action.
d.   What happens in the shot following it? Include the shot size, shot length, audio,
and the screen direction of any action.
e.   Draw conclusions as to the rhythm and pacing of the scene.

3.   Describe the **tension and release** in the scene. How does it serve the story?
4.   Describe the overall **audio design** and how it serves the story.

This exercise will provide the analytical tools you need to really understand the story and
how each shot contributes to the story. The analysis will provide the foundation for you
to not only begin to understand the shots needed to tell a story in a compelling way, but
also how the shots are laid out to tell the story (the placement and length of the shots
that shape the rhythm and pacing of it).

B)   Once you're comfortable with this kind of analysis, apply the same analysis to your own
work. Take the footage from one of your shooting exercises—be sure there's some action
footage—and analyze with the tools in A). Then edit it in order to best tell the story. If
there's not enough footage, shoot more, thinking about the different styles of editing.
Understand how the length of the shot, the pacing, changes the entire tone and energy
of your story.

EDITING WORKSHEET

Similar to the above exercise, but apply it to your own project after you've completed the
script.

1. After completing a rough cut (based on your script), identify the **dramatic core**:

   a. How does the main character emotionally begin the short documentary or scene?
   b. How does this character emotionally end the short documentary or scene?
   c. Where does that change happen? Identify this as the **decisive moment**.

2. Describe the **edit** as it relates to rhythm and pacing:

   a. Describe what occurs in the editing during the decisive moment. Include the shot size, shot length, and any audio.
   b. Describe the action(s) occurring to invoke this change.
   c. What happens in the shot before it? Include the shot size, shot length, any audio, and the screen direction of any action.
   d. What happens in the shot following it? Include the shot size, shot length, any audio, and the screen direction of any action.
   e. How does the rhythm and pacing of the scene feel to you? Is it working?

3. Describe the editing style(s) you use and how it serves the story:

   - Montage
   - Decoupage
   - Collision
   - Linkage.

4. Describe the **tension and release** in the scene. How does it serve the story?
5. How do you use audio to help shape the tension and release?

FOR FURTHER READING

O'Steen, Bobbie. *The Invisible Cut: How Editors Make Movie Magic*. Michael Wiese Productions, 2009. Although an analysis of scenes from fiction films, O'Steen's analysis of these scenes—especially why editors choose certain shots and place them in a scene—conveys a key understanding of the practicality of editing. It includes shots from these scenes, and any documentary journalist should take a look at how pacing is done in works of fiction in order to better understand how to use these techniques in nonfiction.

Pearlman, Karen. *Cutting Rhythms*. Focal Press, 2009. One of the best books on editing, Pearlman in clear prose conveys the theoretical function of the editor, as one who shapes the experience of creating tension and release in the spectator, and lays out the practical tools of how this is done. No beginning editor should be without this book. She puts in words what the master editors do instinctively. If you don't have the instinct for shaping your edit, then Pearlman's book will help you think about why something isn't working and how it can be fixed.

Interlude

Starting Out as a Multimedia Journalist— From an Interview with Angela Morris, Freelance Video Journalist

I started in online video journalism in 2006, right when it was taking off in mainstream media newsrooms. I was the first person at my newspaper, the *San Antonio Express-News*, with "multimedia" anything in her title. My bosses had no idea what I was supposed to do in my job, so I just made it up. At school, they had no idea I would be facing a situation like this— they didn't know what to teach me. So I had to basically teach myself. I started my blog, News Videographer, so I could track all the self-taught lessons I was learning. I watched a ton of online video and I tried to emulate the best. I read what other people were talking about and I tried to implement that advice in my work. I also had the benefit of attending two one-day-long workshops with a television video journalist and a pair of documentary filmmakers, respectively. They taught me a lot of the finer points that make a world of difference.

Today, more and more editors are asking their reporters and photographers to pick up video cameras and produce videos. It seems to be commonplace for journalists to take up this new job responsibility.

After I have a video assignment, I research on my topic by searching story archives and the internet. I call the sources and conduct pre-interviews to get the information I need to figure out the visual images I can shoot to help tell the story. I will figure out when the action or activity I want to shoot is naturally happening and set the date on my calendar. When I arrive at the video shoot I ask the subjects to behave naturally as if I am not there. I will not ask people to recreate activities because I think that is unethical. After the activity is over, or when I feel I have enough b-roll, I will conduct on-camera interviews with the subjects of the story. The telephone pre-interview and research helps me ask questions. Of course, everything I've described only takes place for pre-scheduled stories. My process is different for breaking news! For breaking news I tend to speed, park, run, shoot everything, and try to remember to breathe.

I feel the advantages of being a solo video journalist are that you can better observe the natural course of events because you don't make as big a scene as if you were working with a video crew. You know all the details of the story yourself so you have a better idea of what to shoot and what questions to ask. Since you shot all the video you already have an idea of the story before you sit down at the editing bay.

Working in journalism has allowed me leave my comfort zone. I've gotten to fly in a helicopter, ride a horse, attend street festivals, and more. I got to spend eight months on and off visiting an injured Iraq war veteran and his family as I chronicled what happens in the lives of seriously injured veterans who would have died in previous wars without today's medical science. I covered the funeral of a four-year-old girl whose mother allegedly killed her in a domestic violence situation. The funeral was in a black Baptist church and the preachers were yelling and screaming about the injustice of the situation. In all these examples, I experienced things I never would have experienced if not for journalism. I love that.

My best advice for journalism students today is to learn all the technical journalism skills—reporting, writing, photography, and video—and to implement them through working at student publications and taking summer internships. Get multimedia clips that include stories, published photos, and online videos. Understand: employers hire journalists with these multimedia skills. Also learn to use the internet and social media for reporting and to promote content. I think it's a good idea to learn business and entrepreneurial skills in case you must freelance while you're looking for a full-time journalism job. Most of all, don't give up. Finding a good journalism job is hard, but if you're passionate about journalism and you have the resiliency to overcome a tough job market, it will pay off in a rewarding and meaningful career.

CHAPTER 6

Getting Clean Audio and Crafting a Sound Design

An Audio Workshop with Philip Bloom, Travis Fox, and Wes Pope

INTRODUCTION TO SOUND

As you create your video journalism pieces, do not forget the importance of audio. Without clean interviews—with strong signals—your work becomes compromised. You may shoot great images and put them together in a compelling edit visually, but if your audio is faulty no one will notice the great images you shot. It'll be about the bad audio. You can in fact shoot mediocre images with a decent story and—if you have clean audio—people will watch it.

This chapter will cover ways to capture clean audio in addition to shaping the tone of your work by capturing sounds in the environment you're shooting in (or find the audio you need with audio libraries) and how to weave these strategically into your edit. Sound design is about setting the tone in order to help support the visual tension and release in your video.

It's also important to keep in mind that what you hear is not what the camera hears. Different microphones have different audio qualities and pick-up patterns. It's important to test different microphones in order to understand what each one sounds like, before you go out in the field.

If you're shooting outdoors, be sure to get a good microphone windscreen—a simple foam screen that comes with the microphone isn't good enough. Get a professional-level windscreen—it'll cut out wind noise significantly.

Furthermore, most professional cameras allow you to adjust the levels of the audio, making it more sensitive in picking up audio. Just don't "redline" or clip the audio. If the signal strength is too strong, you'll have useless sound and there's nothing in the editing process that can save this audio. If your levels are too soft, you can boost the volume during editing, but you'll also pick up more noise and hiss, so it's important to keep the levels strong—the meter should read one-half to three-quarters (-24 dB to -6 dB). Less than half and it'll be too weak; more than three-quarters and you may run into the danger of clipping.

Built-in Camera Microphone

Though better than nothing, the built-in camera microphone presents the video journalist with the worst possible choice—ever. It will nearly always deliver subpar audio quality. Never use it unless you have no other choice. And if you have to use it, bring the camera as close to your subject or the action as possible. I don't know of any serious video journalist who ever resorts to a camera mic.

Shotgun Microphone

Most cameras have a shoe mount or XLR microphone input built into the camera. Here, you can attach a shotgun microphone—infinitely better than using the camera's built-in mic. If you're shooting with a DSLR, such as a Canon 5D, 7D, 60D, or a Rebel T3i, for example, you will either need to record audio separately on a digital audio recorder containing XLR inputs (such as a Zoom H4n), or you will need to purchase an XLR adapter for the camera (BeachTek or JuicedLink). In addition, if you want to bring the microphone in closer, you may want to use a "pistol grip"—a way to handhold the microphone to bring it in closer to the subject. These microphones have a cardioid or hyper-cardioid pick-up pattern, meaning that it picks up sound patterns most strongly from the front and the front sides. It's a directional microphone, picking up sounds most strongly from the direction you point it. However, be aware that, if you're more than three feet from your subject, the audio quality will weaken significantly. If you're handholding a camera, bring it in close to capture your subjects' actions and dialogue. A strong signal is important. If your subject is a soft talker, you'll need to bring the mic in even closer (this is why lavs are important) and increase your levels. Always test your levels before recording. Also, if there is a lot of noise directly behind your subject, then it will pick up the sound, so be aware of these noises and move if you have to.

Lavalier Microphone

Typically an omnidirectional microphone picks up sounds from all directions. The lavalier is useful for getting intimate audio from your subject—especially handy during interviews. This also allows the camera and subject to be more fluid, even more so when you're using a wireless lav. The range of the microphone is short, and it is typically wired and attached to a subject's shirt, near their neck.

Handheld Microphone

This is the microphone used by TV reporters. Not really useful for the video journalist who is doing documentary-type work, rather than broadcast news-style reporting. This is an omnidirectional microphone that will get strong, clear audio when handheld by the journalist.

HOW TO GET CLEAN AUDIO

To get the cleanest audio, use a field mixer with a microphone pre-amp, which you can link in to your external digital audio recorder and camera's mic input—in this way, you can not only get a clean signal into your camera, but you will also be recording it on a separate recorder, providing you with a backup in the field.

In addition, make sure the microphone is close to your subject. If you're interviewing someone, put them on a lavalier mic—not only will you receive a clean signal, but the subject can also move around and you'll still pick them up.

If your only solution is a shotgun mic attached to the top of the camera, then be sure your camera is less than three feet from your subject. You want a strong microphone presence and, if you're not close enough, the person will sound too far away, as if they're talking to you from the other side of the room.

Photojournalist and documentary filmmaker Wes Pope says that there are three levels for collecting good audio in the field.

1) Working as a one-man band.
2) Working with an assistant.
3) Working with an audio expert.

Pope notes how "most newspaper work tends to fall in the first or second category," because you're working as a "one-man band." However, sometimes "you're teamed with a willing reporter who may be able to help you in some way, by holding a microphone or boom pole, for example," he explains. The ideal scenario, Pope explains, especially on large projects, is working with someone who records the sound on a separate digital audio recorder along with a "sync-track back to the camera." He's had "opportunities to work in this way on bigger documentaries and commercial jobs and it makes a big difference in what you are able to accomplish. There is a reason why filmmaking is the most collaborative art-form!"

Live action shots, as opposed to interview shots, can be a challenge. "When following live action," Pope says, "we want to attempt to collect the best audio possible by putting a wireless lav mic on our main subject. Take a moment to hide the cords (nothing looks more amateurish than mic cords dangling from your subject)." At the same time, if you're "working with an assistant or audio recordist, have them attach a shotgun mic onto a boom pole to get your mic into the best position possible. Our goal is to collect two separate channels of clean audio in case something goes wrong with one mic (wind noise or clothes rustling, for example)."

For DSLR shooters, check out Wes Pope's "How to Overcome Audio Weaknesses of DSLRs" online at: www.kurtlancaster.com/11/10/2011/how-to-overcome-audio-weaknesses-of-dslrs-by-wes-pope/.

CASE STUDY 1—USING NATURAL SOUND TO SHAPE AMBIENCE IN TRAVIS FOX'S "CRISIS IN DARFUR EXPANDS: TESTIMONIALS"

http://vimeo.com/channels/travisfox#1293941

When you work on your video project, be sure to record the environment you're in, with no dialogue. This "room tone" will allow you to fill in blank spots during your edit. In addition, you can pick up sounds that will add to the ambience of your work. In Travis Fox's "Crisis in Darfur Expands: Testimonials," he shapes an aural environment that not only includes children singing and Abakr speaking, but he also captures the sounds of goats bleating as they walk by, windswept desert sand, and wind flapping the tent. In addition to shooting strong visuals, Fox *listens* to his environment. He records these sounds. He weaves them into his edit at choice moments, helping to shape the ebb and flow of the story.

Fox also takes weaknesses or problems and turns them into a solution. "There are things you have to deal with when you're shooting," Fox tells me in an interview. "Wind is always a problem, so you have to have the proper windscreens, but you can also use it to your advantage." In his "Crisis in Darfur" story, Fox faced a lot of wind, even when he was interviewing a subject in a tent. "I have a windscreen and I try to deal with it, but you still might get wind noise, such as the flaps of the tent, so I actually tried to change it up and use it to my advantage. I focused on the wind noise and I made that an element in the story"— using shots and sounds of the tent flap and a low-angle windswept desert as beats and transitions that enhanced the emotional core of the story (see pictures below.) "So if I'm in the room with someone and there's a fan blowing, typically that would be a distraction, but I'll use it and I'll shoot it and I'll record the audio, and then I'll add that as an element. Then, if you hear it during the interview it kind of makes sense to the viewer and it's not a distraction and it adds to the ambience of the scene."

continued overleaf . . .

My name is Amina Abakr.

Shots from "Crisis in Darfur Expands: Testimonials" by Travis Fox. Fox recorded audio and took shots of windblown sand, as well as a wide shot and close-up of the tent flapping in the wind, so as to add ambience to the scene, while at the same time showing the wind that the audience hears recorded by the microphone.

CASE STUDY 2—USING SOFTWARE LIBRARIES TO SHAPE THE AMBIENCE IN PHILIP BLOOM'S "SALTON SEA BEACH"

http://vimeo.com/10314280

In addition to recording your original audio, you can also use your editing software's audio library of music and ambient audio where you can go in and mix layers of sound to create an ambient experience.

Philip Bloom's "Salton Sea Beach." Bloom used Apple's Soundtrack Pro and files from the Free Sound Project to craft the aural landscape.

Philip Bloom, a cinematographer based in England, shot a poetic documentary work capturing the abandoned environment at Salton Sea Beach, California. He shot it on a consumer DSLR, the Canon Rebel T2i. Rather than record the existing ambient sounds, he used Apple's Soundtrack Pro and the site The Free Sound Project (http://freesound.org) and crafted his own audio design for the piece. The work includes haunting sand, blowing wind, creaking benches, wind howling through walls—all of which provides the aural essence of the environment. Bloom not only captures the visual essence of an abandoned beach town, but the audio environment places us into the space just as viscerally.

Tip: Photojournalist Dai Sugano Inspired by Music

Dai Sugano feels you should learn to tap into your inspiration. Sugano is inspired by music. He'll listen to it in the car. But then he'll go home and turn off the lights and listen to it again. "I can hear a lot more," as the details of the music come out without any distraction. He feels the aspiring video journalist should use such inspiration: "It's just a pure inspiration of listening or watching or finding the movement [in the shot] inspiring, finding that sequence in some videos [when editing] very inspiring. Naturally you will be shooting to get something like that."

Sugano admits being influenced by music videos. In his fashion show piece, "Spring Glow" (2007, www.daisugano.com/Spring_Glow.html), he started by going through his footage, then he listened to hours of sound libraries. "I spent literally over ten hours or more listening to short, short loops. Some are like five seconds, some are like two seconds, and some are ten seconds. So I'm going through and going through and at the same time I'm looking at the video and stills. Some music, some loops are very upbeat with the tempo fast beat—not like melody, it's more like a beat: boom, boom, boom. And I can use that tempo to show my pictures. I learned it from music videos." Sugano is embracing the technology, and, perhaps, since he is untrained in the conventional broadcast journalism style, he's helping to pioneer a new style in video journalism—his visual style influenced by art, photography, and music videos.

CASE STUDY 3—SOUND DESIGN IN WES POPE'S "BILL CAGLE IS A 24-YEAR AIDS SURVIVOR"

http://link.brightcove.com/services/player/bcpid1726686865?bclid=1342091429&bctid=976597402001

Wes Pope, who worked many years as a photojournalist, including stints at the *Chicago Tribune* and *Rocky Mountain News*, among other newspapers, uses DSLRs for his video work. But he is first and foremost a storyteller. Even when working on a fast turnaround project, such as this piece for the *San Francisco Chronicle*, his primary concern is making sure he gets clean audio. "Good audio is crucial to creating an understandable, engaging story," he tells me in an interview. Why? "The brain listens to the story first and you can put almost anything on the screen as long as your audio tells a strong story," he explains. "Audio is 50 percent of video, but in many ways it is actually more than that. There is a saying, 'bad audio plus good pictures equals garbage, while good audio plus bad pictures is called a documentary.'" Although he is being facetious about poor images in documentaries, the point about getting clean audio cannot be understated.

From the opening sequence, we can see how Pope has woven cinematic techniques with audio. In this shot, he utilized a cinema slider (a dolly on a tripod), allowing him to track left to right. At the same time, Pope engaged an eerie sound design that includes high-pitched ringing bells with a lower-pitched "double whoosh" sound. This was a musical piece, "Anaerobica" by PerlssDj.

From the opening sequence of Wes Pope's "Bill Cagle is a 24-Year AIDS Survivor."

Wes Pope utilized an eerie sound design to set the tone for his report.

Music

Do music and video journalism work together? "Music is just another tool," Pope explains. "There are certainly some types of news pieces where it is probably inappropriate, but the Cagle piece was more about creating a mood and reflecting on an anniversary (thirty years since the discovery of AIDS)." But he just doesn't take any song he likes. Reporters must engage in music rights. In the case of the PerlssDj piece, it "was used via a Creative Commons license that allows for commercial uses. I found that particular piece on CCmixter.org (which has a great search tool)." See Pope's tip later in the chapter for a list of free-use music. But be sure that "you understand what rights are granted, that you meet the attribution requirements," Pope adds.

Think about Sound Design at the Beginning, Not End of a Project

Wes Pope feels that you should be conscious of the sound design right from the beginning of your project. Depending on the story, he'll bring certain gear along. "In a basic, quick piece I think about where I am going to get my sound bites," he explains. It's important to control the environment as much as possible, Pope says.

> If it is a man-on-the-street type piece at an event, I come up with a plan for how many people I intend to interview, what types of questions I am going to ask. And you have to start thinking about the audio environment. Is there a quiet place I can conduct the

interviews? A quiet audio environment trumps an interesting background composition in almost every situation. Sometimes the interior of a (not running) car is the quietest place to do an interview. The goal is to gather clean interview audio clear of any background noise—especially no music, which makes it impossible to edit. If you do think you want to hear ambient noise mixed under your interview in some way, gather that audio separately and mix it together in post.

In the Bill Cagle piece, he explains, this wasn't his typical way of putting together a video. But, since he was on a tight deadline, he wanted the work to be more thematic, more "interpretive." He decided to "conduct the interview as audio only, then shoot 'video portraits' of the subject." This allowed him to focus on getting clean audio and then come up with ways to shape poetic video. He admits that video portraits can be a "bit gimmicky (along with the pocket-dolly slider I used in this piece)," but it did allow him to be creative in his approach to shooting. "I know I can make an adequate video if I have a clean interview and maybe a little bit of ambient or music," he explains.

Typically, Pope prefers to "shoot great video interviews, then show them in the final edit as little as possible (only to introduce a character and when there is an emotional reason we want to see him or her—perhaps they are getting choked up or we want to see into their eyes to tell whether they are telling the truth)." He also likes to shoot interviews with two cameras so there can be different compositional choices when editing, making "for more visually dynamic pieces," Pope adds. If you only have one camera, you could move it after each question is answered, but it may cause a distraction to the subject, and interrupt the emotional flow.

Non-sync Sound and Contrapuntal Sound Design

But Pope also loves to craft sound designs for his work. "I am big fan of non-synced sound," he says. This is not to neglect getting good synced audio in the field.

"As shooters in the field we should be working on collecting as much good synced audio as possible (by using wireless microphones, boom poles, and so forth). But when it comes time to edit, I think the magic starts to happen when your audio mix and your visuals start to go in different directions."

Pope says to look at "the opening scene of *Apocalypse Now* or almost any Hollywood film with great sound design."

His approach to this contrapuntal sound design can be as simple as engaging an L-cut, where "sound leads picture or picture leads sound" (we hear someone speak beneath an image, before seeing that person onscreen). Or, Pope says, it can get more complex where you use "any sound-picture-juxtaposition that does not directly match each other. Music, interviews, and ambient audio can all take on interesting roles when they are used in ways to complement or contrast with the images on the screen."

Some may ask if this approach of mixing audio is ethical. Pope feels that only beginners make this "a big ethical sticking point," feeling that approach "is telling a lie. My point is that our viewership is incredibly sophisticated and doesn't get hung up on this point. As long as you are attempting to tell a truthful story to the best of your ability—and your goal is not to deceive viewers—why not make it more interesting and layer your sounds?"

Present-Tense Storytelling

With that said, Pope still feels the best way to craft a story is to get "great audio from a real situation" that provides him with "the potential to make something better than just adequate." He wants to put the audience into the scene as it unfolds—both visually and aurally. "Great documentary storytelling takes place when we achieve 'present-tense storytelling' and we are able to engage our viewers in ways that they are watching real events unfold and they can't wait to see what happens next."

As for the editing process, Pope refers to some advice he was given "early on." "'You can put it off as long as you want, but eventually you are going to have to lock your a-roll [the main interview storyline]. So you might as well get it done first.'" Pope logs his interviews, "and then I get that edited down as quickly as possible. I then start to think about how I want to use music or nat-breaks [natural sound breaks] to bridge between sections of interview." His final step is to "place my b-roll [action footage] over my a-roll and it becomes a jigsaw puzzle. Editing visuals becomes intertwined with re-editing the audio."

Tip: Resources—A List of Online Audio Libraries by Wes Pope

"As I am searching these sites," Pope explains, "any time I hear something I like that has a broad license I download it so I don't drive myself crazy later trying to figure out how to find it again. Create an archive for yourself of pieces you might like to use in the future." Here's his current archive sources:

- ccMixter, http://ccmixter.org/
- Free Music Archive, http://freemusicarchive.org/
- Sounddogs, http://sounddogs.com/
- Soundrangers, www.soundrangers.com/
- Freesound, www.freesound.org/
- Incompetech, http://incompetech.com/m/c/royalty-free/
- Creative Commons, http://creativecommons.org/legalmusicforvideos
- Jamendo, www.jamendo.com/
- Magnatune, http://magnatune.com/genres/
- BeatPick, www.beatpick.com/
- CASH Music, http://cashmusic.org/
- Opsound, www.opsound.org/pool/artist/
- Audiofarm, www.audiofarm.org/
- Netlabels Collection, www.archive.org/details/netlabels.

AUDIO EXERCISE 1

Get a partner and have them blindfold you. Let them guide you to different indoor and outdoor environments. Stand and listen at each stop for at least thirty seconds. Without opening your eyes, notice how your ears pick up a lot more detail in the ambience. Take note of the nuance, the layers of sound occurring in the environment around you.

AUDIO EXERCISE 2

There is no easier way to master audio recording than going out and recording in a variety of environments with a variety of microphones. If you only have one mic, such as a shotgun mic, then test it out in a variety of interview situations until you discover the optimum recording situation. Once you know this, you'll be able to set up quickly and not worry about whether or not you're going to get good sound. This exercise helps you to achieve this.

Interview a subject indoors and outdoors for a couple of minutes. Try the subject alone and try recording the subject in a crowd or space with background noise. Over the course of the interview, adjust the audio levels so that it's weak, medium, and too strong (so you clip the sound).

Also, use the camera's microphone, a shotgun microphone attached to the camera, the shotgun microphone handheld close to the subject, as well as a lavalier microphone attached to the subject. When outdoors, try the shotgun microphone with and without a windscreen. Be sure to state the type of recording you're doing as you record each one, so when you play it back you have the proper reference. In addition, when outdoors, use a lav mic and rotate your subject towards wind and then away from wind. Listen to how the wind can be blocked with the subject's back to the wind.

Next, input your files into your editing software and listen to the sound quality of each. Notice the difference in quality of sound with the different microphones and audio levels. Use this exercise to create your own rules for figuring out how to get the best sound in different situations.

AUDIO WORKSHEET

These worksheet questions will help you think about how to use audio design as a storytelling feature in your project.

- ✧ What audio elements are needed to set the emotional tone of the story?
- ✧ Make a list of these for each section of the story. Identify sound effects, ambience, and music.
- ✧ Are they to be used as audio background for your primary story?
- ✧ What audio elements can you use for transition points?
- ✧ Which of these can you record in the field?
- ✧ What elements do you need to get online using copyright clearance audio libraries? Can any of these be found in the editing software's sound library?

FOR FURTHER READING

"Walter Murch Review," in *The Transom Review* 2005; 5(1), April 1. Downloadable PDF located at: http://transom.org/?p=6992.

Rose, Jay. *Audio Postproduction for Film and Video*. Focal Press, 2008a. Great hands-on techniques for putting your sound through post.

Rose, Jay. *Producing Great Sound for Film and Video*. Focal Press, 2008b. Get the sound you need before going into postproduction.

Interlude

The Importance of Blogging and the Watchdog Reporter—From an Interview with John Yemma, Editor, the Christian Science Monitor

A blog is an easy way to post content online, and that content can be as serious as a 1000 word, fully vetted, sourced story, or it can be as short as one or two paragraphs with a little bit of point of view. So, a blog is just an easy way to post content, and we use them for that reason. We still do online in our web first format, we still do stories that have, that are fully resourced as if they would be for print, and they could be 800 or 1000 words, but we often do blogs because we can get that story up more rapidly. A blog doesn't have to have a casual voice, but because they tend to have a casual voice, they're somewhat more accessible, and you can develop a little bit of a following with a blog, because they're a little bit more . . . almost like you could with a column. There's a little bit more of the personality of the writer that comes through.

You know I think the British have a long history of that kind of journalism. Which is, they don't show you their sources a lot of times, but they try to get it right intellectually. One of the problems with that form of journalism is that you really need to preserve the other form, the old fashioned American form, because it's very seldom that when you have that kind of very knowing and not necessarily on the one hand, on the other hand quoting sources type of piece. It's very seldom that the content of that piece is quoted, you know, because point of view is seldom quoted. What's quoted is the actual document or the quotation, and that's what the—that's the shoe leather work of journalists. So you still have to do that, but you should welcome the other kind, too, and in that whole mix you get a mosaic of storytelling.

All I will say is that the old models of journalism are breaking up, and so the idea even of beat journalism, needs to be preserved. My biggest concern is I think that, you know, organizations like the *New York Times* and the *Washington Post*, and BBC, and the *Guardian*, and the *Christian Science Monitor*—we will continue to cover the world, and we will continue to cover the nation. Where I think there'll be problems is—my biggest concern is that the type of journalism that is not going to get continued support is going to be this beat journalism.

That beat journalism, especially when it's in the seam between national and local. That is, state house type coverage, and local government city hall coverage. Those are beats that are essential to the functioning of democracy, because the watchdog aspect of journalism is necessary there, and I think that's where a lot of disinvestment is really hurting our society. So, I do think that a beat journalist should be an expert if possible. I'm not sure about point of view, but I think that in some ways it's irrelevant whether they have a point of view or not. The main thing is that we have actual bodies who are actually covering city hall and keeping a watch on places like state legislatures that have taxing authority, and therefore have politicians who can easily put their hands into the till, and corruption is an awful problem there. And so far I don't think citizen bloggers have risen to the occasion, but I think it's possible that with enough different types of blogging, and enough different types of journalism, even with mainstream media hurting as much as it is, and maybe good citizen-type wikis, and other things that could be developed, you'll get a new form of beat journalism, a sort of a pro/amateur model, where you have a few professional journalists and a lot of amateur bloggers and citizen journalists. All of them together trying to keep watch on things is a good thing, and so will they be expert, will they be more knowledgeable than their sources will? Some of them will be, but mostly they'll just be committed to watching.

[As for training,] the main thing is critical thinking. If you can do critical thinking, if you can learn how to look at numbers and understand numbers, understand when something doesn't make sense, if you can tell stories and if you enjoy telling stories, then you should have technical training in a lot of different things. Say in video, and framing, and storytelling, but I don't think you need a whole lot of highly technical training in the sense of learning a pure technology, because I think all technology that is used for storytelling is moving toward a point and click, what you see is what you get type of technology.

What's underneath that is the fundamental thing of journalism, which is reporting, curiosity, courage in trying to find something, documenting the evidence, and then telling the story in a compelling way. Those are really the fundamentals, so I would say that you still want those, but you know you want to have technical training to the extent that you can get it, too, so that you'll be able to land your first position. But all of that technology will change over the course of a career in ways that aren't recognizable now. I didn't think there was going to be an internet when I started out in the early 70s as a journalist, and here we are.

CHAPTER 7

The Blogging Journalist
Travis Fox and the Mexican Border Stories

INTRODUCTION TO BLOGGING

This chapter examines the blog created by the *Washington Post* in the summer of 2009, documenting the stories created by a video journalist and the Mexico bureau chief: "Mexico at War: Journey along the Border with Travis Fox and William Booth," (http://voices.washingtonpost.com/mexico/).[8] They engaged in the kind of cutting-edge journalism that'll continue to shift and change in the coming years. Using current technology—the blog—as a framework for journalism containing text, pictures, and video, they at the same time created a space for their audience to add their opinions and stories to the work presented by the reporters. In addition, Fox and Booth tweeted their stories. "The philosophy on this project and Hard Times [the road trip about the state of the economy produced in November 2008]," Fox tells me in an interview in Mexicali, "is that it's kind of wide, but not necessarily deep, and so it's a matter of building an audience as well and interacting with the audience in real time." [9] The web is still in its infancy and experimentation is the name of the game. "So it's just a different way of using the medium," Fox muses.

> I've been at it for ten years, but the medium is still young, and we're still experimenting, so, I think the differences that you see is experimentation. Seeing what works, and seeing what doesn't work, and seeing how to really capture the viewers and involve them in what we're doing.

Become a Journalistic Independent Garage Band

Budding video journalists, as they try to make a name for themselves and attempt to find work either in a full-time position at a television station or an online newspaper, have the opportunity to build a series of videos through a blog site that could not only showcase their work, but also could become a stand-out work. For example, a student could do a series of videos in their community revolving around a single theme, such as homelessness, or create a city hall beat. Don't just make one video story, but create a selection of stories that you'll shoot and edit—and *write* about in a blog. Use the *Washington Post* model. Create a writer–shooter team, if needed. *Become the journalistic expert that others will go to for knowledge they want or need.*

Looking for a job? Create your own job. Become an "independent garage band," says Brian Storm, the founder of the multimedia journalism site, mediastorm.org. "I believe journalism will evolve into at least three camps," explains Storm. There are the ones who work in "the mainstream, in large institutions like MSNBC, the *New York Times*, and Reuters," he tells Andrew Nachison of the WeMedia.com blog (Nachison 2009). Then there's "*The Crowd*"—who Storm says is "basically anyone who has access to the tools of the craft, whether it be a blog or a still camera and a portable recording device." Often these independents are dismissed by journalists, but Storm feels that "more voices and a greater diversity will raise the level of public discourse" and "can ultimately strengthen our democracy"—it will also force journalists "to become better at what we do." The third camp of journalists are the "independent garage bands." Storm defines them as

> groups of professional journalists who collaborate to practice their craft with quality as a focus. They are empowered by the same tools as *The Crowd* and can distribute globally just like the mainstream. The big difference is that they are answering to their audience, not their shareholders.

The rest of this chapter will examine a case study to help you think about how to approach a blog through a real-world example of a professional blog by Travis Fox and William Booth, "Mexico at War: Journey along the Border," a work they produced for the *Washington Post* in the summer of 2009. I will also include a breakdown of Brian Storm's business model for mediastorm.org. It is concievable that a top-quality journalist with strong video journalism and multimedia skills can not only produce work for newspaper sites, but they could also consult with newspapers and businesses needing PR work within the realm of multimedia. As Storm puts it: "*The L.A. Times* is no longer a newspaper trying to make a website work. It is a multimedia production company with great resources. We want to show them, and anyone who will listen, how to use those resources" (Panzer 2008).

If you're not sure how to create a blog, go to www.wikihow.com/start-a-blog

HOW TO CREATE A COMPELLING BLOG OR WEBSITE

- Go hyper-local. Find a niche in your community that is important and isn't being covered. Berkley's Graduate School of Journalism maintains several hyper-local websites covering a variety of communities, one being MissionLoc@l (http://missionlocal.org/). This online newspaper includes a variety of sections (such as Government, Trouble, Business, Education, Art, as well as including video). You could team up with several other journalists and create a business model using such sites as a model to draw inspiration.

- Become the expert. Many journalists specialize and not only maintain a variety of contacts who are experts in the field of their passions, but journalists can become the ones who know a lot about a particular specialty. Perhaps you become known for landing good shots and interviews with local sports participants, or you're an expert in the arts, or you're tapped into the local government scene. Master an area, cultivate your sources, and present the stories that you and the community care about.

- Present your best work. Don't put up stories that are weak. Even if you've done a good job shooting the video, but your story doesn't feel complete or you recorded bad audio for some reason, take the extra step and fix these, even if that means you need to reshoot.

- Keep your site clean; don't clutter it. The more information and sections you have, the more content you'll need to create. Focus on a few and let them be your strongest work. Keep the design clean.

- Be passionate and maintain integrity. Don't get sloppy in your reporting. Dig deep and report the truth. Return calls and emails in a timely fashion. If you make a mistake, correct it and be honest about it. If you want to be perceived as a professional, then act professional.

CASE STUDY—BLOGGING THE DRUG WAR IN MEXICO WITH TRAVIS FOX AND WILLIAM BOOTH

Finding a Story on *Narcocorridos* in Mexicali

It's 9:00 p.m. on a Friday night in Mexicali, a city of a nearly a million people just across the border from Calexico, California. The eighty degree Fahrenheit evening cool feels good after a daytime high of 104 and the desert Santa Anas whip dust through the air as I tightly follow video journalist Travis Fox through the streets. With him are journalist William Booth, the *Washington Post*'s Mexican bureau chief and their translator, Arturo Chacón. They're not too hard to follow, as Fox is driving a red SUV with Colorado plates, rented Stateside. They're looking for *mariachi* who perform the *narcocorridos*—drug ballads, the folk songs of praise to the drug cartels. And these journalists haven't eaten since lunch.

Less than two hours earlier, they checked into the Siesta Real Hotel on Calz. Justo Sierra Avenue, got directions, jumped into showers, then hit the ground running. They've been driving all afternoon from Sasabe, Arizona, where they looked at a "virtual fence," a multi-billion dollar radar to sense border crossers. The day before, they were in Nogales—a town with more border traffic than LAX—where they interviewed President Obama's "Border Czar," Alan Bersin. Fox and Booth don't slow down and I'm hoping I don't have to run a red light and get pulled over by Mexican police. At one point Fox yanks his car over to a gas station to get directions. Then they pull over again and talk to a woman walking by. She gets in the car with them, a willing navigator along the back streets of Mexicali. We finally arrive along a strip of road along

Plaza de Mariachis, where dozens of *mariachi* performers stand and sit by their cars on both sides of the street—a vague Mexican echo of the Modesto streets of George Lucas's *American Graffiti* (1973). They're waiting to be hired. Fox, with Arturo's help, talks to one group. Booth wanders off, finding his own leads. He later returns, and a one-hour conversation ensues. Although Arturo holds a tripod and Fox has his video camera bag strapped over his shoulder, the equipment stays put. They're gathering information, not shooting until they have their right subject.

Fox explains, "We probably spend as much time talking to people and being directed to a certain area and finding things out as we did actually letting the camera roll, so that's what reporting is. That's what we do." The performers hand out business cards. Fox and Booth are looking for a bar where they can find performers to shoot. They've been on assignment since Saturday, June 13, 2009, starting a border road trip in Juarez and planning to end in Tijuana on Sunday, June 21. Along the way they're talking to police, citizens, drug czars, and ranchers as they get the feel for the lay of the land in Mexico's drug war. They're writing blog entries and posting either video or photos at each of their stops, as they Twitter their way to an interactive audience. It's the new way for online newspapers to gather a readership and build a community of loyal followers. "They send in suggestions," Fox says, "and they're good suggestions."

> You get a mix of crazy people writing, to be honest. But then you also get a lot of really good suggestions. You'll find someone just write in and they tell about their personal experience. Someone who lived in El Paso, saw our videos, [and it] brought back memories of how it was to live on the border, and people share that, and it's really refreshing to see that, and then someone takes the time to see that. People also wrote in questions for us, and [shared] their thoughts. And then, for example, when we interviewed the new Border Czar a couple days ago, we relayed those questions and we asked him directly. And then that will come back on the site. So it's really a matter of involving the users, and we're trying to do that with this piece more and more.

But before anything goes online, the interactivity is face-to-face, reporters being reporters whether the end product is a print story or a video blog.

Distinguishing Information for a Notebook, Blog, and Camera

The interactive experiment may be new for journalists working in the online field, but Fox is learning how to distinguish between the information needed in a notebook, for a blog, and on camera. "If you have hours [of video] full of information that you're not going to use in the piece, but is good reporting, then it just slows you down in the edit." He learned his lesson from the early days (1999) when he was starting to shoot video and had too much footage to meet a deadline. "Now I feel like I'm able to get the information I need in my notebook before I even start shooting," Fox comments. It's the on-the-ground reporting he did in Mexicali. He'll use the notes to "narrate the pieces, and then I'll record the interviews for the quotes that I need." With "daily deadlines, if you shoot too much and if you have too much material, that can limit you. Another mistake that beginners make."

Fox is no longer a beginner. His documentary on Hurricane Katrina victims, "Living in Flooded New Orleans" (2005), earned him an Emmy Award, and most recently his short doc,

"Hoping for a Miracle amid the Rubble"—about the Sichuan earthquake in China in 2008—earned Best Web Video from the National Press Photographers Association in 2009. And in the streets of Mexicali, Fox and Booth have teamed up to discover how the drug culture has spread to the folk songs, the *narcocorridos*, as I get a behind-the-scenes view of professional reporters at work.

The two hour journey to find a bar described earlier translates to the sixty-two word second-paragraph blog entry:

> We swing by the Plaza de Mariachis, where dozens of bands have pulled their vans up to curb to await customers looking to hire some musicians to make a party. Manuel Delgado of Los Zorros tells us "the town is dead." We ask where we might hear some music, especially the ballads about drug lords, and he points us to La Conga (Fox and Booth 2009a).

Their on-the-ground reporting pays off. They're directed to a bar, and we hop in our cars and pull up in front of La Conga, a bar in the shape of a boxcar, not too far away from the Plaza de Mariachis. But we have cameras and the bouncer prevents us from entering. Fox, through Arturo, asks the bouncer if he can film inside the bar. The bouncer calls the owner on a mobile, and we're let in. The owner, Daniel Angulo, is operating the bar tonight. It's after 10:00 p.m. and the *mariachi* are playing their heart out, as the music overwhelms the dimly lit tiny bar filled with clientele listening to the music and partying.

Mariachi in a Bar

Fox and Booth talk to different customers as Fox tries to figure out who to shoot. He knows he wants the band, and at one point he brings the camera close to the performers. There's no stage. Fox crouches down low, entering their personal space as he shoots a low angle of the singer. He'll hold the shot for some time, before turning the camera, handheld, to another musician. He surreptitiously shoots customers at a table, then later shoots them dancing. During the musician's break, he interviews them, translating through Arturo. He picks up an interview with another customer. Well after midnight, we step outside and Fox says he's starving, and he, Booth, and Arturo wolf down tacos from a nearby sidewalk vendor as they debate whether or not to return to the Plaza de Mariachis and interview more singers. No money is passed to the vendor until they have eaten their full. They agree to return to the place and shoot another band willing to sing to them and record interviews on tape. They get back to Siesta Real Hotel at 1:30 a.m.

The evening would net them a 532 word blog entry and a two and a half minute video. It would begin, however, with a Tweet from Fox at 7:35 a.m.: "Today—finally!—we hit the bar! Join us for a drink and a 'narco-corrido.' http://tr.im/mexbor #mexborder." The video shot at the plaza would not be used. Fox wanted to keep the focus of the video story on the bar, while the blog text would contain story elements from both the bar and the Plaza de Mariachis.

Although Fox has earned awards for his work, he doesn't consider himself a documentary filmmaker. He doesn't like the word. "I like documentaries. I watch them. But when describing my own work, I never use the term." He considers himself a journalist, and he joked earlier how much easier it would be to just write a story. Indeed, he considers shooting and editing video as a type of writing.

> I look at what's in the *Washington Post*, in the newspaper, and I look at what I do, and I feel like it's the same information. And I feel like if I'm going to take an article, say an article that Bill [Booth] would do, here, and if I were to adapt that into video, then what I'm doing is what it would look like. You know it has a strong character, and there are some differences, obviously. Mine's more character-driven, in video, but the information is the same, so I don't feel like there's a big distinction.

Indeed, he says later in the interview that video is a form of writing: "I think especially for a younger generation, people who grow up with video [realize that] producing a video, editing a video, making a video is not any different from writing. It's literally that easy. And when we have more people doing it, we'll have greater diversity" of stories and shooting styles. Shooting and editing video is not as easy as writing, but Fox's point should be heeded, for today's generation raised on multimedia a video is a form of text, treated as text, and perhaps utilized more than written texts.

As more and more journalists adjust to the age of multimedia reporting online, Fox's words become wisdom when considering the process of creating stories for the web.

Writing the Blogs

Let's examine the first entry to Fox's and Booth's blog to see how the *Washington Post* conveys cutting-edge journalism as they experiment with blog elements. Published on Monday, June 15, 2009, "Addicts Latest Victims of Drug War," presents the story of Guadalupe Martinez, a heroin addict in Juarez, who stands beneath the bridge connecting Juarez to El Paso, Texas. "Thousands of people stand in line for hours waiting to walk into the United States," Booth writes in the blog. "As they wait, Martinez stands down in the riverbed and shouts for dollars and pesos, and the crowds, bored, throw the money down. They laugh as Martinez and other homeless alcoholics and addicts run after the fluttering bills."

The top of the page contains a banner title, "Mexico at War: Journey along the Border with Travis Fox and William Booth," the Mexican flag image looking like it's flapping in the breeze (Fox and Booth 2009b). The design is clean and simple. It sits below the main page header of the *Washington Post*, which contains a series of menu buttons from news to classified ads, as well as a search window. To the right of the blog sits an ad. On the top left of the page, we see in small print: "Sign In" and "Register Now"—users cannot post feedback on any story without registering and signing in. Three ads sit on the upper right, center top, and far right of the blog. Below the central ad, the *Post*'s links and search window sit. Below this we see the banner title for "Mexico at War" blog, and below this is a Google map featuring the Fox–Booth journey across northern Mexico, interactive hyperlinks placed where they've visited and written and shot stories.

From here, we get a 300 word explanation about the project:

> The border between United States and Mexico is the land where straight lines blur, and where two national cultures collide and collude. The writer Alan Weisman, author of

La Frontera, called the borderlands "the most dramatic intersection of first and third world realities anywhere on the globe." There is a lot of good on the border, and these days, plenty of bad. The border is a militarized hot zone, where tens of thousands of Mexican soldiers are fighting a vicious drug war against well-armed, rich and powerful drug traffickers, who smuggle across these desert highways 90 percent of the cocaine so voraciously consumed in the United States. On the U.S. side, the federal government is pouring taxpayer money into the border, promising to stem the flow of cash and guns heading south, while the border patrol continues its ceaseless cat-and-mouse search for Mexican migrants sneaking north.

We're setting out to drive the borderlands from Ciudad Juarez, across the river from El Paso, to San Diego's sister city Tijuana. Along the way, we're going to tell the stories of overwhelmed small town sheriffs, of drug smugglers and drug czars, of the Mexicans who struggle to survive in dusty villages and the Americans who fear that the drug war is getting way too close for comfort. We're going to talk to cops and mayors, some scientists and singers, and lots of regular folks, too. We've got a map, an ice chest, a video camera, and the laptops. We've got some stories planned but we also would like to hear from you. What do you think about the drug fight along the border, and what it is doing to the people? What dots on the map should we make sure to hit? Please let us know in the comments section below. You can also join the conversation on Twitter by using the #mexborder hashtag.—William Booth and Travis Fox

It's a tight introductory text, meant to grab the attention of their potential audience, the interactive reader-viewer. The first paragraph is designed to set up the poetics of the piece, revealing the writers' style and providing a context as to why they're chasing stories along the border, citing Weisman's words: "the most dramatic intersection of first and third world realities anywhere on the globe." They frame their intent with words that hit the hot spots of contemporary news—"The border is a militarized hot zone, where tens of thousands of Mexican soldiers are fighting a vicious drug war against well-armed, rich and powerful drug traffickers, who smuggle across these desert highways 90 percent of the cocaine so voraciously consumed in the United States." This is followed by how US taxpayers' money is being spent to help stem the flow of immigrants, north, and guns, south. We see the controversy being set up, helping to feed a lively and interactive discussion. The second paragraph maps out their intended plan, with an appeal to participate: "What do you think about the drug fight along the border, and what it is doing to the people? What dots on the map should we make sure to hit? Please let us know in the comments section below. You can also join the conversation on Twitter by using the #mexborder hashtag."

The invitation for interactivity leads to feedback and story ideas by participants. The first post, occurring on the morning of June 15 by a user posing as "alance," notes: "The more the border becomes militarized (on both sides) the greater the risk becomes and the greater the profit becomes. The biggest tragedy is the danger to innocents who get caught in the middle of this war." This is followed by a post ("weds30"), who writes (with numerous typos): "be sure to stop in palomas mexico which is directly across the border from columbus n.m. i was raised 45 miles from there and will be extremely interested in what your impression is . . . i remember it 50 years ago with fondmess". Fox responds to the poster: "We are planning a stop in Palomas . . . stay tuned!" There's also one post about legalizing drugs to help stem the violence, with another participant feeling that the legalization of drugs will lead to more addicts. The debate helps feed the energy of the stories Fox and Booth will do.

Focusing on the site and how it offers interactivity with the map, users can zoom in and out of the map as well as click on the blue mini-balloons that indicate where Fox and Booth reported their stories. Clicking on one of the balloons in Juarez, a pop-up window appears on the map listing the title of the story, "Addicts Latest Victims in the Drug War." Clicking on the story link in this pop-up window loads the particular blog entry, which, in this case, contains a video and the blog text.

The blog entry is short—less than 300 words. It's not designed to convey a full news story. However, when placed in context with Fox's video, we get a bigger picture. The text on its own doesn't give us the full story; neither does watching just the video give us enough information to fully provide us context. The two complement each other. In the text story we see the traditional story hook:

> When you visit the drug rehab centers in Ciudad Juarez, what you notice are the arms. The addicts have arms that are purple with scars. The new guys have arms still raw from the needles. The counselors, former addicts themselves, have scars that are fading away, faint but still there (Booth and Fox 2009).

This story is about addicts, and the words pull us into the story, needles being a strong image that engages the readers' emotions.

The second paragraph takes it a logical step further—the addicts are being murdered: "A few weeks ago, gunmen burst commando-style into a gray cinderblock building where 60 patients were bunking down for the night. The assassins killed five. Motive unknown." This material is not in the video, but, when we see the video, this text deepens our understanding of what the character is facing.

The third paragraph discusses the reporters' visit to the center, and they describe the evidence of the murders: "a young man reluctantly let us in." He "pointed to a spot on the floor, where we could still see the blood. That's where his uncle died." Again, none of this information is in the video, but it expands the story and provides more depth, in a style of storytelling that Fox admits is "kind of wide, but not necessarily deep."

The fourth paragraph introduces Guadalupe Martinez, the subject of the video, who says that it is dangerous on the streets: "He was in another rehab center three months ago that closed after drug gangs threatened an attack, and now he says there are more junkies on the streets than ever." The final paragraph provides a description of the video:

> In the video above, Martinez fights for his fix by begging for money below the international bridge that connects Ciudad Juarez and El Paso, where each day thousands of people stand in line for hours waiting to walk into the United States. As they wait, Martinez stands down in the riverbed and shouts for dollars and pesos, and the crowds, bored, throw the money down. They laugh as Martinez and other homeless alcoholics and addicts run after the fluttering bills.

This paragraph, and the blog entry itself, provides the contextualization for Fox's video, the visual and aural storytelling record that helps place the audience into the scene of the border town of Juarez.

As one interactive participant commented on June 15, 2009:

> In that final shot, his face says it all—the helpless look of an addict.
>   Mexico—the new Columbia. And we ignore it at our own peril. The US needs to engage much more forcefully here than practically anywhere else. May be this can be contained now—but if this goes unchecked, like the violence against treatment centers, it is akin to ignoring the rats/mice/termites scurrying around at our doorstep.
>   Soon, you will find them inside.
>   Btw, fantastic video. Thanks.

A controversial statement that makes reference to the final shot in the video, and congratulating the reporters for the good video, but the implication of the text in reference to rats/mice/termites resonates with the US air of superiority. It's a reference the reporters would never write. But, in the world of an interactive audience, people's opinions resonate with their own personalities unfiltered by an editor. It provides color, extending the story into the minds of the audience, and then they process it and provide feedback, revealing their values, desires, and opinions about the story produced by Fox and Booth. Fox feels that this is one of the key components of the video-blog storytelling experiment for the *Washington Post*: "It's a matter of building audience and interacting with the audience in real time."

Video Blog: "Addicts Latest Victims of Drug War"

The video is the heart of the blog piece—Fox's signature composition and strong exposure taking us into the emotional life of the addict as Guadalupe struggles with his addiction and we learn how the drug cartels are targeting treatment centers—perhaps so as not to lose customers for their illicit drugs. Without the video, without the images and audio that situate the audience into the scene witnessed by Fox and Booth, the text blog would lack panache, as well as visual documentary evidence. Filmmaker as witness. The video is short (2:09), containing twenty-two cuts, but it encapsulates one of the main issues dealing with the drug war, and it would promote a lively discussion among the audience who participated.

Below, I provide a transcript of the story, along with a frame from the first second of each shot.

The narration is tight, providing just enough information to give us context. Fox chooses the shots that are visually strong, providing a visual progression for the story, shot by shot. His central character, Guadalupe, provides just enough screen time for us to see his desperation, Fox capturing it through video and audio.

Fox's edits shape the narrative around Guadalupe's desire—which in this case is the need to beg for more money so he can feed his heroin addiction. Again, the classic story structure, even in such a short piece, provides the emotional arc so common in cinematic storytelling. Notice how, in context with the blog text, the video becomes more rounded. The information about five people murdered at a shelter, as we're told in the blog, with written evidence of a man pointing to where his uncle was killed, deepens Guadalupe's story as he explains how the drug treatment center he was attending was shut down due to threats from the drug cartels. The fourth paragraph of the blog does tell us about this, but with both pieces of evidence—the shooting written down as text, the other spoken on camera by the subject as documentary witness—which makes us believe his story that much more.

1.

In Spanish, we hear Guadalupe shouting up to the bridge.

Fox: This is home for Guadalupe Martinez, . . .

2.

3.

. . . the paved-over Rio Grande, the border between Ciudad Juarez, Mexico and El Paso, Texas.

4.

5.

In Spanish, we hear Guadalupe shout up to the bridge, begging for money.

6.

Fox: He spends his day begging for money from the long line of people waiting to cross into the U.S.

7.

Guadalupe (in broken English): I need 70 Pesos more. I got $2.50, American. It's 30 Pesos Mexicanos. I need 70 more to make a hundred.

8.

Fox: Each day all he wants is one hundred pesos, or about eight dollars.

We hear natural sound of wind blowing and Guadalupe counting money softly to himself.

9.

Guadalupe: Heroin. Heroin. That's what I buy. Heroin.

10.

Fox: Three months ago, Martinez was in rehab and perhaps on the road to recovery.

11.

Martinez shouts up to the bridge.

12.

Fox: But then suddenly his treatment center closed.

13.

Gaudalupe (voice over): We got a telephone threat saying we'd be killed if it doesn't close.

14.

Fox: As the drug war continues unabated in Juarez, some drug treatment centers are shutting down after being shot up or threatened by the cartels. And Guadelupe says that means only one thing:

15.

Guadalupe: Everybody's in the street because all the centers are closing.

16.

Guadalupe: Everybody's in the streets. Everybody's in the bridge, everybody's in the . . . you know (grunts).

We hear people scuffle around, trying to catch money thrown down to them.

17.

Someone picks up change from the ground.

18.

Fox: Competition is becoming fiercer, . . .

19.

. . . especially when dollar bills are dropped.

The camera pans and follow two men struggling over money.

20.

Camera zooms in to two others fighting for dropped money.

Guadalupe: I've been trying to stop taking drugs . . . and to live in peace without drugs . . . and start a new life.

21.

Fox: But Gaudelupe's hopes might have to wait a little bit longer . . .

22.

. . . until the violence here in Ciudad Juarez eases.

Travis Fox creates a series of compelling images of Guadalupe begging for money from the El Paso and Juarez Border Bridge.

From this story, we discover a larger story—not about drug addiction, but about life in El Paso and Juarez, a story that would never have been heard in a public forum if the *Post*'s blog didn't allow for audience interactivity. From a post by "JBC1," June 15, 2009:

Thank for you doing this series. I am a native El Pasoan now living in the DC area. My family still lives in El Paso and my mother and brother-in-law work for immigration and customs. I think that the way of life on the Texas-Mexico border is very hard for outsiders to understand. The border is not as rigid as many think. People go back and forth and families and the economy are dependent on this fluidity. My 84-year old grandmother still drives herself to Juarez once a week to see her sister. She also goes to see her dentist and get her hair done. Even though we have asked her not to because it has gotten so dangerous, this is what she has always done and she can't imagine life another way. The drug war has definitely changed the way of life in El Paso and all along the border. I hope that you will get to see the beauty and the spirit of border life and not just the effects of the drug war. These terrible times are relatively recent and I hope that someday, whether through legalization or better enforcement, the border will return to the culturally rich and beautiful place that I knew.

This person's story is thoughtful and presents a reflection of what daily life on the border is like, and what the nostalgic past was like before the rise in drug use and the drug war. For some, such as this person's grandmother crossing the border once a week, they continue as they have always behaved: "this is what she has always done and she can't imagine life another way."

But we also see a larger debate, again presenting a thoughtful argument, by the person who posted comments right after JBC1. This one is by "constitutionalcitizen," who argues how the war on drugs should be "The War on Addiction," making the case that "Addiction is a physical illness. Because the target organ is the brain, that simple fact gets lost." The commenter also feels that the reporters are wasting their time with "'ain't it awful' stories about addicts and drug cartels in Mexico which only sensationalizes the criminal activity over exploring public policy in support of a solution."

The journey Fox and Booth take covers police being outgunned, a ranch, the use of a virtual radar-based fence, and how citizens try to take back the streets of Juarez. This participant judged the entire project with their first story, which helps set up one facet of the drug problem—addicts being targeted, a story perhaps not heard about before by the *Post*'s audience.

Thirteen Blogs

Fox's and Booth's week-long journey through some of the border towns of northern Mexico would yield thirteen blog stories, seven videos, and eighty-seven comment posts by readers (as of the morning of July 6, 2009). The stories include the first one analyzed above:

Ciudad Juarez: "Addicts Latest Victims of Drug War" (text and video)
Ciudad Juarez: "A Rare Night Out in Juarez" (audio music with 360 degree photo panorama)
Ciudad Juarez: "A Drug Smuggler's Story" (text and video)
Palomos: "The Town of Lonely Dentists" (text and video)
Ascension: "A Small Town Cop, Out-Gunned by Traffickers" (text and video)
Cajon Bonito: "Restoring Natural Life on the Border" (text and video)
Los Corrales: "The End of the Road" (text and panorama)
Nogales, Arizona: "Show and Tell With the New U.S. Border Czar" (text and video)
Nogales, Arizona: "Tunnel Network Ends Border Patrol Underground" (text and photos)
Sasabe, Arizona: "Virtual Fence Gets a 'Do Over'" (text and photo)
Mexicali: "*Narcocorridos* and Nightlife in Mexicali" (text and video)
Tecate: "A Dangerous Route North" (text and video)
Tijuana: "The Law of Unintended Consequences" (text and photo).

It's a bold experiment and it is too soon to tell if this kind of journalism will pay off. As Fox explains, "I think every few years you get kind of the killer app, or the thing that's going to save newspapers. And one time it's video and the next time it's something else." He admits that "advertising on video is more lucrative, period," but he also realizes that "the numbers don't tend to be as high as articles, and that could be because they have a thirty-second ad in front of them, I don't know." In either case, he also feels that video alone will not save online newspapers. "I don't think there's anyone who thinks reasonably that video is going to save newspapers, that's not going to happen." Yet, doing new kind of journalism for web-based newspapers is imperative, Fox believes.

> As we focus more and more on the web, we need to produce journalism for the web, on the web's terms, and what that means is greater interactivity with the readers, that means video, that means interactive graphics, that means all of the above.

Tip: Brian Storm Builds a Business Model by Engaging Audience Feedback

Brian Storm, founder of the successful journalism startup mediastorm.org, explains how their success is modeled not by random viral-fed videos on youtube.com, but on a conscious business plan that involves their video and slideshow publication website, sales and syndication, production and consulting work, as well as their multimedia workshops for journalists.

Storm, in an interview with Professor Steve Weinberg of the Missouri School of Journalism, explains how their website "is the soul of the company. It's the place where we have the most freedom to innovate. We have over 130 countries hitting our website each month. We've built a global audience in a very short time period" (Weinberg n.d.; all quotations by Brian Storm in this section are from this source). Storm believes that the website can gain money through "advertising, sponsorship and transaction. We can support three premium sponsors and we're currently sponsored by the *Washington Post*." He feels that "Madison Avenue" is looking for "rich media" advertising that "will support a new era of journalism," because they "want to place video ads but there isn't much top-tier content to place it against." Quality work that attracts numbers will attract advertisers. They also allow users to buy DVDs of their work or "buy the book related to the documentaries on our site"—they get sales figures when users are directed to Amazon.com from their site—even if they're purchasing other items on Amazon. Furthermore, Storm syndicates their work "to broadcast and websites around the world. We share those licensing fees 50/50 with the journalists and artists that we collaborate with in producing the pieces."

Because the people who work for MediaStorm have such high-quality knowledge of production techniques and storytelling, they also produce works and consult for other companies—the third way Storm is able to bring money in to the company. "What I want you to think about is that *National Geographic* is not just a world-class magazine, it's a media company. So 'Ivory Wars' can show on television, on the web, and in the print magazine. That's what we're trying to do, create an opportunity for people to see stories in multiple media, multiple formats," Storm explains to Professor Weinberg.

And their fourth item on MediaStorm's business plan involves what Storm refers to as their "evangelism"—he wants other journalists to learn about their approach and share it with the world. "We're teaching people how to report with distribution multiple media and formats in mind," he says, "and how to package the reporting afterward. Our workshops are really about sharing our methodology and we have a ton of fun as well as you can see from the behind the scenes piece that we produced at our New York City workshop (http://mediastorm.org/workshops).”

It's also important to tap into the social networking phenomenon of Web 2.0, such as creating a Facebook page for fans, who not only may comprise your friends, but people from all over the world as they discover the quality of your work. “Once people find us they subscribe to our newsletter or our RSS feed which drives 35 percent of the traffic to our website,” Storm muses. “This is another reason it's not important for us to publish on a regularly defined schedule. Our readers come back when we have something new and we use a variety of ways to keep them in the know.”

A journalist working in today's environment can't just shoot video and write a blog. They must build an audience and interact with them. Focusing on a beat, becoming an expert in a particular area will help make you stand out. Don't try to become an expert in everything. Stay focused. You may want to stay local, becoming an expert in your community, so people will know to come to your site for the information they want or need.

EXERCISE IN BLOGGING

Find a blog in the field you want to write and produce video for. Analyze it. What elements work for you? What doesn't? How is the writing used? Identify the “about” and “bio” pages and describe how they make you feel. Do you feel like you're on a site that's conveyed professionally? How is video incorporated into the stories? Make a list of the qualities of not only the content, but also the design.

BLOGGING WORKSHEET

These questions will help you set up a blog as an independent journalist. In short, you want to define a beat and create a blog. In order to begin as a video journalist—if you can't find a job right away or if you want to start creating a portfolio while studying, then take a look at the community around you. Find something you're passionate about and tap into it. Go out and find a set of stories revolving around a single theme. Perhaps you can create a cutting-edge sports beat, capturing games and conducting interviews with players. Perhaps you'll cover an arts beat. Or you can cover city hall, the homeless, or even a particular neighborhood. Find the characters and tell their stories. Create the blog and start posting your material online, including written material, when needed.

✦   What are you passionate about? Make this a starting point so you will continue with the project through tough times. If you don't care enough about the project, will your audience?

⬧ List the experts in this field you respect. Find others that *they* respect.

⬧ Pre-interview some of these for your story. Identify story potentials and characters they mention. Start extending the pre-interviews and research to these other characters, whether they're experts or potential subjects to shoot.

⬧ Map out potential stories from these interviews and take note of particular characters that could become central characters for each. Email them, talk to them, meet them. Start building trust with them.

⬧ Once you've determined the potential of your project, create your blog with a title that conveys a strong theme for it. Write a clear mission statement describing what the project is about. Write a professional bio.

⬧ Write and/or shoot these stories, and edit them, and post them online.

⬧ Post a link to each blog on Twitter, Facebook, and other social networking sites.

⬧ Share links to your stories with experts, fans, and media outlets that might be interested in the story. Get yourself known as an expert in the field!

FOR FURTHER READING

Martin, Gail. *30 Days to Social Media Success: The 30 Day Results Guide to Making the Most of Twitter, Blogging, LinkedIN, and Facebook*. Career Press, 2010.

Conclusion
Creating Your Own Stories

Many may rue the day newspapers went online and bemoan the loss of print dailies dropped on their doorstep by paperboys and girls as part of their morning coffee reading ritual, but the floodgates have opened and we can view more information than we could ever need or want online, including video journalism. We need good journalists (writing, audio, and video) in order to tell the important stories. We may laugh at the "bad kitty" videos on YouTube, or gloat over some celebrity mishap, but these are not stories important to our society.

With the demise of print papers, what have we lost and what are we gaining?

On the surface, we may have lost the paper held in our hands—but not really. I have the Sunday edition of my *New York Times* delivered to the doorstep on Sunday mornings. I receive the weekly print edition of the *Christian Science Monitor*. I also read articles from these papers—among others—online nearly every day. With iPads and laptops, people can read online stories and watch videos wherever they go. Indeed, the reading experience on my iPad entails a better experience for me than turning paper pages. Through the glass touchscreen interface I engage a unique tactile response while reading and I have dozens of newspapers and magazines at my fingertips.

What I don't do is watch the evening news—a ritual I grew up on. I rarely even watch the online editions of the daily news, whether local or national.

Yet, I do watch *Frontline* and, in the recent past, *Bill Moyers Journal* online. I watch videos produced by the *New York Times*. I go to Bob Sacha's website: http://bobsacha.com/video/, Brian Storm's site: www.mediastorm.com, Wes Pope's www.wespope.com, Travis Fox's http://travisfox.com, PBS's *POV*: www.pbs.org/pov/, Adam Ellick's www.adambellick.com, Dan Chung's www.dslrnewsshooter.com, Jonah Kessel's www.jonahkessel.com, among others. These sites indicate that some of the best visual journalism occurs outside the conventional production sites of broadcast news.

Furthermore, many of these video journalists putting out strong stories tied to strong visuals are shooting with hybrid DSLRs—photography cameras that shoot cinematic-quality high-definition video. Travis Fox shoots video for *Frontline* with a

Canon 7D. The fact a student journalist can purchase a Canon Rebel T2i for around $600—and shoot better images than video cameras costing thousands more—cannot be understated. The tools of strong visual storytelling are possible for reporters working on a tight budget. When I consulted for the *Christian Science Monitor* in the winter and spring of 2008, we had about $1500 to spend for camera gear for each reporter. We purchased consumer HD cameras (JVC and Panasonic)—little cameras you can hold in the palm of your hand. They worked for what they needed to do. However, with the release of HDSLRs (Canon's 5D Mark II announced in October 2008), these cameras have revolutionized the independent film community and they're beginning to impact how news is shot. Dan Chung shoots most of his packages on DSLRs. He trains video journalists on how to use these cameras. Photojournalists at the *Arizona Republic* in Phoenix provide video support for the local TV news station at *12 News* (www. azcentral.com/). Go online to the equipment page (kurtlancaster.com) of this book and check out some of the gear. Regular prosumer video cameras don't cut it for me anymore. I see their images as inferior.

But getting a camera isn't enough. People can shoot really bad video with the most expensive camera and some can shoot really nice looking video with an inexpensive camera. In order to get better at video journalism, journalists need to take into account the cinematic possibilities of the video camera—whether it's a prosumer camera costing $6000, $3500, or a $1200 Canon 60D (as many of our multimedia students use at Northern Arizona University's School of Communication). They need to understand and begin to master the purpose of different lenses, shot sizes, camera angles, depth of field, as well as getting proper focus, color balance, and exposure. And on top of all that, getting clean audio is imperative. It's a lot easier to just grab a notepad and a pen and talk to people to get the story. Writing is much easier than shooting and editing video. The video journalist's pen is the camera, their ears an audio recorder, their writing style is crafted with Final Cut Pro, not Microsoft Word. They must master the technology before they can really start telling good stories. The technology must become second nature, just as writing becomes second nature for a reporter writing a story.

This book has hopefully provided some of the tools to help place you into a strong position for thinking about story structure, character development, and a basic knowledge of shooting cinematically and editing for pacing and rhythm. Although the broadcast news and documentary styles are vastly different in how stories get delivered, they're essentially the same—a nonfiction story told in a compelling way in order to capture an audience. If you want to develop a story with more character development, then let the characters speak onscreen more often and shoot compelling images that visualize the story. If you want a story where a lot of information can be conveyed quickly, then write more narration with video images used as support. My preference is to try to get into the story visually and craft a compelling story rooted in a character's words.

In the end, it's you and your characters and the stories you craft through them for an audience. If you're honest with yourself and with them—and you've mastered the technical skills needed to do it well—then your audience will become enriched by your stories. If they become a better person, a better citizen because of the job you've done, through the story you've told, then you've become what a good journalist should be: those who tell the stories of our time, setting an accurate record in a compelling way.

Future historians and citizens of the world may look back at our record of civilization. What will this record look like? Will it be a civilization bombarded with sensational news stories designed to increase ratings for a network or will it be stories expressing a deeper meaning about the human condition?

In other words, do you want to look back on your career and be the one who spun stories for Fox News or sucked an audience in with sensational crime stories on CNN? Or do you want to be the one who told the story of a struggling artist during a recession, crafted an interview witness of atrocities in Darfur, shaped compelling images of poverty in India, examined how a woman stood up for her rights as a mother and independent woman in China, explored the impact of the drug war on the border towns of Mexico, and presented the story of a twelve-year-old girl wanting to receive an education in Pakistan?

I wrote this book for those interested in telling the personal stories, the stories that tell the larger picture of our civilization through the examination of individual people whose lives may seem minor in the scale of the world, but they're the ones who move the world forward, behind the scenes, the ones who make up the lifeblood of communities, the ones who give their all to help make the world a better place to live.

And be sure to check out the website at http://kurtlancaster.com/ in order to get the latest updates on equipment, interviews with video journalists, and additional tips.

Afterword

New Voices

I wish this book had been written five years ago so I could have skipped all the hard learning I did—reading, practicing, talking with people who knew so much more than me, then trying out new ideas and failing and failing again.

I much prefer to ride along with the cast here, wonderful storytellers all, and to absorb the tools, techniques and tips they have been kind enough to share with us.

Kurt has gathered it together in a logical, lively, comprehensive, and compelling form that even taught an old dog like me a number of new tricks and new ideas.

So, what comes next?

Now that the tools have become democratized and affordable—the average cellphone can capture and upload video that can be instantly broadcast around the world and could help foment a political, social, or personal revolution—what sets us apart as documentary journalists?

Stories.

We're no longer just the cameraman or photographer, we're now the storyteller. With this new freedom and power come new challenges and responsibilities.

We need to think about the story, not just the visuals. Working in the time-based medium of video/film can be a challenge for us, since we are well versed in looking for the single perfect moment frozen in time. Now we're looking for what some call an "extended moment." We can't just be satisfied with a single image; we need to capture a series of shots, a great scene or sequence to tell the tale.

Audio and video bring a new set of ethical concerns and complications that don't often fit into the black and white ethics rules formulated over the years when print reigned. It's even easier now to slant a story, to skew an opinion and make black seem white using these new tools. Just because we have a blog and a camera doesn't mean we can say whatever we want. We have to be true to the story, to tell it well and represent our subjects fairly. Transparency is key.

What about stories?

This web revolution is a great opportunity to go back to the source material of great storytelling. We crave stories. The psychologist Carl Jung thought stories sprang from deep inside of all of us and were shaped by the same hidden universal rules. That's why fairy tales share many common threads across cultures.

But as *Video Journalism for the Web* points out so very well, relying on the tried-and-true (and tired) way of telling stories is not going to cut it. Facebook and Twitter are but the flick of a finger away if our attention fades, even for an instant. Web storytelling has to have a fast start and a one-on-one feel.

Universal and compelling narratives will always get people's attention. Experimental techniques, new and surprising ways to tell a story, can finally be celebrated.

We need to start paying attention to our audience. I don't mean pandering to them but always asking these questions:

- "Why should they care about this story?"
- "How can I connect this story to them personally?"
- "How can I surprise them with something new?"

For instance, what can the twenty-five-year-old heroin addict in my story, a world away physically and emotionally from my audience, teach them about their lives?

If the only reason we think our audience should watch our stories is that we think our stories are important and "they should care," well, our audience will be gone to social media in a flash.

I don't need to see another story that reinforces that idea that the world is a sad and depressing place, something that I already know too well. Relying on guilt to force people to watch stories doesn't work.

I certainly don't mean that we should avoid serious issues that might seem sad or depressing. But we need to see those stories in a new way that can tap into that intense well of universal ideas and connections that are deep inside all of us. If we don't take that challenge, there are too many other places on the web to go to get that fix.

Not only do we need to engage our audiences, but we also need to think about new ways to make them a part of our storytelling. In a way they are already: the instant response of social media means that people will call us out if we stray or if they think something is unfair. And the other side is that people will instantly Tweet, Facebook, email, or spread our story through social media if they like it, allowing stories to be exposed to a massive worldwide audience, instantly.

Now that we have the skills and tools and stories from this wonderful book in our hands, and with the new powerful freedom of the web, it's up to us to go out and find these compelling and universal stories.

So surprise me with something new, teach me something that I can take into my own life, show me the world in a way I've never seen it before.

The world is waiting.

Bob Sacha
Freelance multimedia journalist
aboard Turkish Airways flight 001 bound for New York City, August 4, 2011
http://bobsacha.com

Notes

1   For sake of shorthand, I will use broadcast news, television news, cable news interchangeably, since they all share a similar style in presenting news—and I'm referring to the short news pieces found at local stations, as well as CNN, for example.

2   The cinéma vérité style doesn't typically use narration, so I consider the Ellick–Ashraf piece a hybrid of this form.

3   This interlude is drawn from an interview that first appeared on the www.DocumentaryTech.com blog (Lancaster, 2010).

4   Koci-Hernandez, Richard. Interview with Dai Sugano. *MultimediaShooter.com*. Accessed July 1, 2009. www.multimediashooter.com.

5   Yes, I know cinematography refers to film and cinema and videography to electronic video, but in the 21st century digital filmmaking is increasingly becoming the norm and cinematographers use high-definition cameras to "paint with light." I therefore define these two terms differently in order to differentiate the average video shooter from the documentary journalist.

6   The interview has been edited for clarity.

7   There are multiple tutorials on learning how to use editing software as a tool. This book is not a handbook on how to learn video editing software. (If needed, there are also many tutorials online.)

8   The *Washington Post* has since taken down this blog, but lessons and stories generated from the project remain an important historical document of how newspapers experiment with this form. Furthermore, in 2010, Fox left the *Washington Post* and became a freelance video journalist, producing work for *Frontline* at *PBS*. See his video journalism work at: http://vimeo.com/travisfox/. Furthermore, the blog site is no longer active on the *Post*'s website—it is archived, but the video links do not work. The videos covered in this chapter are located at Fox's Vimeo page: "Addicts Latest Victims of Drug War," http://vimeo.com/5525320 and "*Narcocorridos* and Nightlife in Mexicali," http://vimeo.com/5828646.

9   All quotations by Travis Fox are from interviews conducted by the author in July 2009, unless otherwise cited.

References

Aristotle (n.d. [350 BCE]). *Poetics*. Translated by S. H. Butcher. Accessed June 16, 2011. http://classics.mit.edu/Aristotle/poetics.1.1.html.

Artis, Anthony (2007). *The Shut Up and Shoot Documentary Guide*. Focal Press.

Bernard, Sheila (2007). *Documentary Storytelling*. Focal Press.

Block, Bruce (2008). *The Visual Story: Creating the Visual Structure of Film, TV, and Digital Media*. Focal Press.

Booth, William & Fox, Travis (2009). Addicts Latest Victims of Drug War. *Washington Post*, June 15. Accessed August 1, 2009. http://voices.washingtonpost.com/mexico/2009/06/about_this_project.html.

Fox, Travis. (2010). Emmy Award-Winner Travis Fox Ventures into the Cinematic Journalism Debate. *DSLR News Shooter*, June 15. Accessed July 7, 2011. www.dslrnewsshooter.com/2010/06/15/emmy-award-winner-travis-fox-ventures-into-the-cinematic-journalism-debate/.

Fox, Travis & Booth, William (2009a). *Narcocorridos* and Nightlife in Mexicali. *Washington Post*, June 25. Accessed August 1, 2009. http://voices.washingtonpost.com/mexico/2009/06/narcocorridos.html.

Fox, Travis & Booth, William (2009b). About This Project. *Washington Post*, June 12. Accessed August 1, 2009. http://voices.washingtonpost.com/mexico/2009/06/about_this_project.html.

Hampe, Barry (2007). *Making Documentary Films and Videos*. Holt Paperbacks.

Hollyn, Norman (2009). *The Lean Forward Moment: Create Compelling Stories for Film, TV, and the Web*. New Riders Press.

Junnarkar, Sandeep (2007). Building a Perfect Storm of Journalism and Multimedia. *OJR: The Online Journalism Review*, January 22. Accessed August 6, 2009. www.ojr.org/ojr/stories/070122junnarkar/.

Koci-Hernandez, Richard (2009). Interview with Dai Sugano. *MultimediaShooter.com*. Accessed July 1. www.multimediashooter.com/wp/uncategorized/podcast-on-assignment-with-dai-sugano/.

Lancaster, Kurt (2010). Shooting in Haiti: An Interview with the Renaud Brothers. *DocumentaryTech*, February 8. Accessed December 29, 2010. http://documentarytech.com/?p=3489.

Lancaster, Kurt (2011). *DSLR Cinema: Crafting the Film Look with Video*. Focal Press.

Malkiewicz, Kris (1986). *Film Lighting: Talks with Hollywood's Cinematographers and Gaffers*. New York Prentice Hall.

Mamet, David (1992). *On Directing Film*. Penguin.

Martin, Gail (2010). *30 Days to Social Media Success: The 30 Day Results Guide to Making the Most of Twitter, Blogging, LinkedIN, and Facebook*. Career Press.

Mercardo, Gustavo (2011). *The Filmmaker's Eye: Learning (and Breaking) the Rules of Cinematic Composition*. Focal Press.

Nachison, Andrew (2009). MediaStorm: Story, Art, Passion, Purpose. *WeMedia.com*, April 14. Accessed July 29, 2009. http://wemedia.com/2009/04/14/story-art-passion-purpose-mediastorms-brian-storm/.

O'Steen, Bobbie (2009). *The Invisible Cut: How Editors Make Movie Magic*. Michael Wiese Productions.

Panzer, Mary (2008). Photojournalism for the Web Generation. *Wall Street Journal*, July 8. Accessed July 29, 2009. http://online.wsj.com/article/SB121547603666334187.html.

Pearlman, Karen (2009). *Cutting Rhythms*. Focal Press.

Pitzer, Andrea (2010). Travis Fox on NPR/Frontline collaboration: 'I feel like it's a great model for the future.' *Nieman Storyboard*, April 16. Accessed June 14, 2011. http://niemanstoryboard.us/2010/04/16/travis-fox-on-nprfrontline-collaboration-i-feel-like-its-a-great-model-for-the-future/.

Rabiger, Michael (2009). *Directing the Documentary*. Focal Press.

Rabiger, Michael (2005). *Developing Story Ideas*. Focal Press.

Renaud Brothers (2011). http://renaudbrothers.com.

Rose, Jay (2008a). *Audio Postproduction for Film and Video*. Focal Press.

Rose, Jay (2008b). *Producing Great Sound for Film and Video*. Focal Press.

Sugano. Dai (2007). Interview. *MultimediaShooter.com*, May 11. Accessed July 2, 2009. www.multimediashooter.com/wp/uncategorized/podcast-on-assignment-with-dai-sugano/.

"Walter Murch Review" (2005). *The Transom Review* 5(1), April, 1.

Weinberg, Steve (n.d.). *Reynolds Journalism Institute Online* (rjionline.org). Accessed July 29, 2009. http://rji.missouri.edu/centennial-professors/storm-b/index.php.

Wu, Chrys (2009). 10 Golden Rules for Video Journalists. *Ricochet*, January 10. Accessed June 16, 2011. www.chryswu.com/blog/2009/01/10/10-golden-rules-for-video-journalists/.

Index